PRIMAL WAY
and THE PATHOLOGY *of*
CIVILIZATION

PRIMAL WAY
and THE PATHOLOGY *of*
CIVILIZATION

By Walter Robinson, PhD

iUniverse, Inc.
Bloomington

Primal Way and the Pathology of Civilization

iUniverse books may be ordered through booksellers or by contacting:

iUniverse
1663 Liberty Drive
Bloomington, IN 47403
www.iuniverse.com
1-800-Authors (1-800-288-4677)

ISBN: 978-1-4759-2913-3 (sc)
ISBN: 978-1-4759-2915-7 (hc)
ISBN: 978-1-4759-2914-0 (ebk)

Library of Congress Control Number: 2012909890

Printed in the United States of America

iUniverse rev. date: 06/14/2012

CONTENTS

INTRODUCTION TO THE WAY

Indigenous people the world over share common values and core philosophies. Much of this is rooted in a shared experience of being in the Natural world. As a species our nature is informed by millions of years of primate evolution. As organisms functioning in the environment we must develop ways of living that are ecologically sustainable. All organisms must find their ways into ecological niches that sustains the well-being of life. In more recent times cultural patterns have led humanity toward ways that are not sustainable and that are extremely destructive of the Natural world. Moreover, it is not just a question of survival, but also the quality of life. Humanity has become, in its political behavior and social dynamic, extremely cruel. We have seen acts of genocide, exploitation, endless wars, and other such acts of malevolence, and this against a backdrop of nihilism and discontent. It would seem that the world has lost it way, and so we may wonder whether life was better during past times and if it can be that way again.

Myths of a "golden age" are quite common in high cultures throughout the world, but for indigenous people who existed, or still exist without having been impacted by high-cultural civilization, no such myth was called for. The high-cultural pattern emerged about six thousand years ago displacing the older indigenous ways as it introduced urbanization, hierarchical political systems, economic class divisions, and the development of written language. Indigenous people know of a Way of life full of meaning and well-being. Among the American Indians there is the notion of the "original instruction," which is a spiritually based ecological wisdom that set the norm for how to live a good life. For Indians and other indigenous people like the African Bushman and Australian Aborigines, Nature is sacred and there is a proper Way one must live in the presence of the sacred. This is called among the Indians of North America the Way of Great Harmony. For many American Indians, as well as other indigenous people, this Way is a living tradition. This wisdom is common to all humanity in-so-far that if we trace our roots far enough back into history we all find our indigenous ancestry. For the Europeans this past is all but lost with the virtual extinction of pagan religions. In China the indigenous wisdom entered into the history of that civilization as the philosophy of Taoism. And as Taoism found its place in the culture of China, it formed a critique of civilization.

Philosophical Taoism is a normative system of understanding through which one may perceive the state of health of any given society. It is radically different from all other systems of normative philosophy that have developed within the high-cultural systems of civilization in that it is not based on anything that can be explicitly stated or otherwise known with a conceptual mind. In the normative philosophies of civilized thought there are standards by which judgments may be made as to what is right or wrong. According to Taoism, standards of thought that allow for moral judgments are problematic at best, and more often than not they are pathological. The Tao, or to translate into English, the Way, has no standard by which to make judgments; rather, it allows for a way of seeing that yields deep penetration into the nature of any given situation. It is not an intellectual construction, but a way of wisdom that transcends intellect.

It is my position that, viewed from the perspective of the Way, civilization is seen as pathological; on the other hand, primal cultures like those of the Bushmen and Pygmies of Africa, and the Australian Aborigines, along with other similar indigenous people, are seen as mostly healthy. I further assert that systems of normative thought based on the values of civilization are incapable of solving the pathological conditions that they have created. For healing it is necessary to recover the Primal Way. Without the Way it is not possible to have a workable normative philosophy that is not subject to the relativistic complications that exist in civil ethics and historically defined moralities. Arguments are endless. What is needed is healing that goes beyond arguments.

The facts of cultural relativism have become the grounds for the assertion of moral relativism. It is clear that what one culture holds as "good" can be seen as "bad" by another. Values vary from culture to culture, and it is often inappropriate to judge the behavior of people in one culture according to the standards of a different one. There are those who believe that insofar as cultures are products of human activity, their values are likewise, thus there is nothing outside of this relativity with which to base any normative judgment. Furthermore, there is no ultimate reason to believe in any values at all, thus one is free to existentially live according to whatever values one will, or to value nothing at all. Such a position means that "anything goes" without limits.

Moral conservatives argue against moral relativism, asserting that if one has no standard upon which to judge the moral conditions of societies then there are insufficient grounds to condemn fascism, slavery, genocide, and other such forms of tyranny and immoral actions. One must either say that the Nazis may or may not be judged as bad depending on the value system one holds, or that there is something that is transcultural and transhistorical upon which to base judgment of the kind that can condemn certain behavior independent of the cultures in which it happens to occur. In the position that is articulated as the theory of Natural Law, it is asserted that there exits a morality that is not an artifact of human invention, but that is true in its own right. With Natural Law ethics it is believed that the moral originate from God or something equivalent, and becomes revealed to mankind though religion. The problem here is that people disagree on matters of religion and on interpretation thereof, much less as to whether or not God exists outside of human imagination. Also it is difficult to understand moral justification for inquisitions, holy wars, political oppression, sexism, racism, and much more of the same that have been advocated in the name of religions.

The more philosophically oriented moral thinkers will point to rational principles as a guide to ethics. In the philosophy of Plato it is asserted that there is a moral order to life, that one may know it through reason, and at the level of pure being reason is that moral order. Reason has become to moral philosophy in the West what God is to monotheistic religions, asserting that reason precedes the phenomenal world and is eternally fixed. The problem here is that to believe that reason is eternally fixed is to make an irrational leap of faith. Also, there is nothing about reason that can tell a person how to live apart from some pre-existing set of values. Reason can clarify what is, but cannot say what ought to be. Thus reason is often valueless, except for its own sake in relationship to whatever is presupposed. For example, rational humans have used reason to invent atomic bombs and other horrible things⌈The reality is that humans do not do what they do so much in accordance with reason, instead they invent reasons for things that they do.⌉

A different kind of moral philosophy based neither on religious dogma nor on rational principles can be found in ancient China. This philosophy is based on the Way of Natural Virtue. One lives the Way of virtue by living in harmony with Nature. A basic assumption in Chinese philosophy is that Nature is good. Humans as part of Nature are likewise good. Needless to say not everything is always good. Chinese philosophy explains that Nature is in a constant state of change; things may from time to time fall out of harmony, but the tendency is to recover harmony. There is no need to know the good, only to live it by living life to its fullest. There is an innate moral sentiment that actualizes itself with the fullness of living in harmony with Nature, and this is the Way of Natural Virtue.

The Chinese philosophy of the Way has aboriginal roots. Most tribal people living in indigenous cultures the world over understand and live by the wisdom of the Way. These people see the health of both the individual and the tribe in terms of harmony with Nature. American Indian philosophy, for example, centers around the teachings of Great Harmony. This teaching is wisdom of deep spiritual ecology, which is symbolized in the image of the Medicine Wheel. The Medicine Wheel is the Circle of Life and the cycles of Nature. The ultimate ground of Life and Nature is the Great Mystery. It is the Way in that everything is because of the Great Mystery. The Way is with everything and nothing is apart. This philosophy is not so abstract, for it is based on the experience of Nature. By this I am saying that the philosophy of the Way is not a construction invented by mental activity, but an aboriginal understanding of that which is most basic to Nature.

China is one of the oldest continuous civilizations in the world, but its social matrix is based on earlier patterns that emerged from the Fertile Crescent region and the Nile Valley about six thousand years ago. This cultural matrix diffused outward and arrived in China about four thousand years ago. Before the advent of civilization most of the world's people were living in Neolithic villages. Life in these villages was egalitarian based on a clan system in which everyone was part of an extended family system of sharing and caring. The philosophies of these people were based in harmonizing with the Natural world, but the civilized people had a different way, the way of patriarchy, which is about conquering Nature. In other words, civil ethos is about conquest. Civilized order is about hierarchical control, with a chain of command like a military organization. It is held together with force and violence. It justifies its existence with philosophies and religions that are derived from invented abstractions and are superimposed on people through authoritarian indoctrination. Pure primal experience of Nature is labeled evil. Thus civil ethos cuts itself off from Nature and perpetuates itself out of fear of wild Nature. As it spreads, it transforms peaceful societies into warring states.

The themes of Western religions have much to do with conquest. The universe is seen as a war of good against evil. Nature is viewed as the domain of evil, and as such, must be conquered. The mentality of the modern world is based on the theology of conquest transfixed into the paradigm of technology. The consequence of this is the ecology crisis. What underlies this crisis is a psychological disposition driven by an ethos that is out of harmony with the aboriginal Way. Modern humanity has lost the Way, and now seeks to fill the sense of loss by pursuit of material wealth. The more modern people pursue material wealth, the more off-center they become, with the consequent feeling that life is meaningless and absurd. To escape this feeling people then pursue more and more materialistic endeavors, but only succeed in adding more and more layers of the same creating even more extensive alienation compounded into a vicious cycle.

The modern world is a violent place. Millions of humans have been murdered in the name of nationalism, idealism, religion, or just plain greed. Vast amounts of resources and energy have been devoted to weaponry. The power to kill is the measure of political power. Governments depend on their military. Much of the world economy runs off the military-industrial complex. Economic life itself is a kind of warfare—one company pitted against other companies, one product against another, businessmen struggling to win over others, and so forth. This competitiveness is reflected also in sports and education. The whole modern world exists in struggle and violence, driving humanity to madness. Murder, suicide, rape, alcoholism, drug abuse and psychological disorders have tended to increase year after year, decades on end with no end in sight. The modern world is the greatest tragedy in human history.

A society can be said to be healthy only to the extent that the people who live within it are healthy. Psychosocial healthiness is inseparable from happiness. Thus, a major indicator of whether or nor a society is healthy is whether or not the people are happy. If the people are killing each other and themselves, destroying health with drugs and alcohol, indulging in excessive behavior that disrupt the environment in which we all live, and treating one another with cruelty and indifference, then the people cannot be said to be happy, and the society is thus sick.

To heal we must transcend the social conditions that cause the sickness and thereby gain vision of health. As the old saying reminds us, "the blind cannot lead the blind." Those who are heavily conditioned by the pathos of civilization have not the vision to lead humanity into health. Some elders within the traditions of shamanism have healing wisdom. The keepers of the old Ways understand the disease of the psyche, but modern humans for most part are too blind and arrogant to learn the Medicine. An old Chinese proverb says, "Only when one is sick of sickness is one opened to healing." Perhaps the intensity of the pathos of modernity has led humanity to this point.

The Way of healing is in the very fiber of our nature. The question is how to awaken it. Essential to using the Primal Way as a normative perspective is awakening to one's true nature. Intellect is insufficient. Cultivation is what is needed. Methods of cultivating the Primal Way begin with emptying the mind. This is much like Zen. One does not literally empty the mind; rather one finds a quiet core of consciousness that is nondual and exists prior to thought formation. One then centers into this quiet core and disengages identification with the thoughts that arise. One then views the world as one with this quiet core and from this wisdom is spontaneously born. In some ways this is like phenomenology, except for the absence of subject/object dichotomy, and nondependency on analysis. Phenomena are seen and allowed to be seen for what they are without the mind projecting itself upon what is seen. No mental activity is needed in order to have understanding. When one uses mental activity to understand phenomena, one does not understand phenomena; rather one sees mostly the activity of the mind. When the mind is quiet, phenomena may "speak" for themselves, and then it may be known what is or is not healthy. No judgment is needed. Indeed judgment is a kind of mental activity that can obstruct wisdom. With true seeing there is just seeing, and what is seen is true beyond words and concepts.

One of the major problems in the social sciences is the tendency of investigators to project their values onto the social phenomena they study. There is no way of using the mind that can solve this problem. But if one can transcend mind even as one uses it, then one can view social phenomena in a way that is free of bias. This does not negate values; rather it is based on those values that are transcultural and transhistorical. It places value on the process of life in accord with the Way.

The wisdom of the Way may at times place one who is in accord with it at odds with social norms. In some aboriginal cultures the shamans often live on the fringes of the society. Even so these aboriginal sages are concerned with the well-being of the people. The more pathological the society, the more outside of society the sages will appear to be, whereas in a healthy society the sages will be fully integrated. Primal cultures are governed to a large extent by the wisdom of these sages. The health of the culture depends on that which the healing art of the shaman brings to it. The shamanic sages as such practice normative social psychology in the way they affect the people. In a techno-industrial society a sage would be a dropout; in an aboriginal society a sage blends in as to appear ordinary. In so saying this I am asserting that aboriginal societies in their original form are healthy, and modern society is not.

Ruth Benedict, an anthropologist who devoted many years to studying indigenous cultures, developed a normative anthropology based on the notion of synergy. A high-synergy society is one that is healthy and holistic; a low-synergy society is one that is fragmented, oppressive, aggressive, greedy, and the like. The word "synergy" refers to the behavior of a system as a whole unpredicted by the parts considered separately. Modern society is one in which individuality is accented, and in such a society the individuals feel alienated and isolated, and the culture is fragmented with little in the way of a sense of common good. It is low-synergy because there is little in the way of a feeling of belonging. In a high-synergy society, people have the feeling of belonging and they find real benefit in being in relationships with others. Wealth tends to be more communal and used more for the common good.

Humanistic psychologist Abraham Maslow synthesized Benedict's application of the notion of synergy with his notion of self-actualization to develop a normative social psychology. For Maslow self-actualization is central to any understanding of mental health. A high-synergy society is one in which self-actualization is supported and facilitated. A low-synergy society is one that produces conditions that result in psychological deprivation and alienation. Taking Maslow's notion of self-actualization and modifying it to actualization of the Way, I find a point of reference around which to explain an aboriginal normative philosophical psychology. A high-synergy culture is one in harmony with Nature, wherein people benefit from the health of actualizing the Way. A low-synergy society is one in which there is disharmony with Nature, the consequence of which is sickness. Most of the best examples of high-synergy culture are to be found among aboriginal societies.

Cultural anthropologist Margaret Mead's study of Samoa moved her to a conclusion that Samoan culture is healthier than Western civilization. Her study focused on adolescent adjustment in Samoan society wherein the transition from childhood to adulthood is smooth. This tends to be true of aboriginal societies that are undisturbed by modern civilization. In Western society adolescence is turbulent. Youth educated according to Western models often experience emotional problems. Sociological information suggests that this condition has gotten progressively greater over time. Juvenile delinquency, alcohol and drug abuse, violence and suicide have become progressively more commonplace experiences of youth over the history of modernity.

The Westernization of Samoa brought with it the problems of the West. When Mead did her study in the 1920s, suicide was all but nonexistent, whereas by the mid-1980s Samoa had the highest per capita suicide rate of any country in the world. There were also increases in domestic violence, alcoholism, crime, and the like. Lowell Holmes, a cultural anthropologist who carried out studies in Samoa after Mead's, points out that this increase coincides with the impact of Westernization on Samoa, whereas those areas least affected are still much as Mead described them. My own experience in Samoa leads me to agree with Holmes. Similar phenomena exist among the native tribes of the Americas. Indian elders tell me of a time when the tribes were healthy, and they describe how they witnessed the degeneration as Western ways entered into their culture. The Indian communities that have done best to preserve health are the ones that resisted Western impact on their core values.

Among many tribes of the Americas there is a practice called the "Vision Quest." This Quest is often used as a rite of passage from childhood to adulthood. It is believed that in order to be a fully integrated adult member of society and Nature, one needs Vision. One common way of Vision Quest consists of going into a Sacred Power place for a time (usually four days and nights), fasting and praying for Vision. The praying has a meditative effect in focusing the mind, stilling and emptying it. When consciousness is thus opened to Nature, the Great Mystery is revealed. Another means of Vision is the use of Plant Teachers such as Peyote, Psilocybin, or Ayahuasca, among others. Vision is the normative perspective that shamans use in order to comprehend the nature of sickness and to reveal the means of healing. In my own Vision from Peyote with the Native American Church, and then from Ayahuasca with Shipibo Indian shamans of the Amazon, I have come to know the meaning of Harmony with the Way. As I returned to techno-industrial society, I found that it is inconsistent with my Vision of Harmony. Over the years I have viewed the modern West in terms of my Vision in some effort to understand what has gone wrong. Most of what I find is consistent with the perspectives of American Indian sages like Black Elk, Lame Deer, Crow Dog, Paula Allen, J.T. Garrett, Marilou Awiakta and many more. In addition to these there are feminist like Mary Daly, Merlin Stone, Barbara Walker, Riane Eisler, Elinor Gadon, and others who reveal and unveil the neurosis of patriarchy and the Wisdom of the old Ways.

Vision of the Great Mystery entails wisdom of Great Harmony. The wisdom of this Vision yields eco-spiritualism—Nature is sacred, and Self is one with Nature. There is no self-actualization apart from Deep Ecology, for there is no self apart from Nature. The Native American philosophy of Deep Ecology is symbolized as the Sacred

Hoop, articulated as the Medicine Wheel. The two great Powers of the Wheel are Earth and Sky, which manifest through Nature as male and female. The harmony of male and female is the most essential attribute of Great Harmony. It seems to me that there is no single indicator more symptomatic of the pathology of civilization then male violence against females. This is violence against Life itself and extends itself into environmental exploitation, yielding ecological disaster. The Way of Great Harmony places prime importance on Life and the female principle of giving life. This is not so much given as a concept as a fundamental insight of Deep Ecological Vision.

My method of inquiry is unorthodox as judged by a traditional Eurocentric mode of academic scholarship, and it must be this way when we consider the nature of the subject at hand. The Way is holistic and realization of the Way is transcendental to intellect. Traditional scholarship in the West is intellectualism compounded by more intellectualism—hence it cannot comprehend the Way. The Way does not exclude the use of intellect, but before one can use intellect in harmony with the Way, one must first move beyond it to contemplate the tranquil of Non-being. This tranquil seeing is the first principle of Taoist epistemology. Traditional modes of intellectual inquiry are part and parcel of the sociopolitical power structure that perpetuates pathology. Intellectualism is a product of patriarchal oppression and has historically been used to justify the status quo and to administer its affairs. It is impossible to approach the Way in terms of this tradition because the tradition is incompatible and inconsistent with the Way.

It is my intention to express Taoist philosophy in a fashion that is compatible and consistent with the Way. I assert that the Way is not a historical invention, but a discovered reality with philosophical roots in aboriginal consciousness. I present Taoism in synthesis with American Indian philosophy, with the assertion that they are speaking of the same truth. I then view the conditions of civilized ethos as an outsider looking in and describing what no insider is able to see if he or she is so predisposed as to identify with it and stand in denial of its effects. There can be no cure without overcoming denial and confronting the disease. This is an inquiry that intends to unveil the core of civil ethos. This is radical philosophy to undo the history of philosophy and lead the reader to Primal Suchness; and with it the cure will come of itself.

The structure of this work is as the weaving of a comprehensive gestalt. This weaving approach reflects the nature of the Way. The web is woven as the development of a Vision. The structure of the Vision is the Medicine Wheel. The axis of the Wheel is the Power of Earth and Sky, which teaches the need for harmony of male and female. The Wheel turns on the four seasonal directions: East, South, West, and North. Each direction symbolizes a mode of being. These modes parallel the Chinese five-element theory. The East is Wood, which is Spring. This is the place of giving birth. The South is Summer, which goes with Fire. This is the place of family and community, and of intimacy of warm feelings. The West is Fall, which goes with Minerals. This is the place of coming of age and entering into Vision. The North is the place of Winter that goes with Water. This is the place of Knowledge. The four directions come from the Center, which is the element Earth—the Primal Mother.

Moving past this introduction, this work is divided into five parts corresponding to the directions of the Wheel, and coming to center at the end. We will begin in the East to give birth to our subject. Next we will move to the Sacred Hoop of the South to give a family context to the subject, following this to the West in which our subject will come of age, and then with ageing comes the knowledge of the North. We will conclude by bringing it all to center.

THE WAY OF THE EAST: GIVING BIRTH

Patriarchal civilization has been in existence for about six thousand years—this against a backdrop of more than a hundred thousand years of human existence. As such, patriarchal civilization is relatively recent. Moreover, it is a radical divergence from previous social conditions. It is my contention that this divergence is pathological.

Prior to the advent of patriarchal civilization, patterns of culture tended to be gynocentric. By this I mean that femaleness was (and for many tribal people still is) of central religious concern. In the primal worldview of gynocentric cultures, the Universe is seen as a living being. So 'being' implies birth, and birthing is a female function. Thus, it is understood that insofar as life comes from the female, the Universe as a living being is of female origin. This femaleness is equivalent to Nature. Nature comes from herself to herself though the act of creation. She is, as such, the creator. Life gives life to herself though this act of self-creation, which is the act of birthing. In this way of understanding, femaleness is prior to maleness and is the all-inclusive origin of the web of existence. She is, as known in the Navajo mythos, Spider Woman who weaves the world from her own body. In the old mythos, the mother is first, and then she creates out of her body a male consort. Maleness exists within the context of what is given by the Great Mother.

This primal worldview—the prevailing mythos for most of human existence—was militantly overthrown and displaced by a different way of understanding. About six thousand years ago the Indo-Europeans began a massive military migration. They were a people who worshipped sky gods. Their social structure was hierarchical and required obedience and loyalty to the power

1

structure. For them the Earth was not sacred, but reduced to a thing of property. In a similar manner, women were reduced to the status of human cattle. Femaleness was thus reduced to an inferior and subservient position under the power and authoritarianism of the sky gods, who were, by and large, male.

With the aid of the war chariot the Indo-European sociopolitical pattern spread like cancer. Often non-Indo-European people, like the Semites, Egyptians, and others, took on the Indo-European pattern, thus contributing to its spread. About four thousand years ago the Chinese learned the use of the war chariot, and with it the sociopolitics of patriarchy.

Prior to the Ch'in dynasty (221 B.C.), village life in China remained more or less gynocentric. Patriarchy was a social pattern of the imperial courts and the military. After the Ch'in dynasty, patriarchal Confucianism became the official state philosophy, and was culturally superimposed on village life, thus eroding gynocentric values. On the other hand, Taoism became the philosophy that preserved these older values. Gary Snyder in *The Old Way*, writes: "Taoism being, following Dr. Joseph Needham's assessment of it in *Science and Civilization in China,* the largest single coherent chuck of the matrilineal descent, mother consciousness-oriented, Neolithic culture that went through the so to speak, sound barrier of civilization in the Iron Age and came out the other side halfway intact. Thus, through its whole political history it has been anti-feudal and anti-patriarchal . . ."[1]

The Chinese word "tao" translates into English as "way," and as a philosophical notion it means the Way of Nature. The Chinese notion of Nature is that which "happens of itself" or "self so." The aim of Taoism is harmony with Nature. This harmony is entered into by way of going with the self-happening of Nature without effort, or effortless action. What is entailed in this teaching is that Nature being that which is so of herself, to be in harmony with her is to be as she is, thus without effort. Harmony is like self-generative homeostasis. All one needs to do is center oneself on the Way, and without effort harmony comes about of itself.

---

[1]   Snyder, *The Old Ways*. 38.

The Taoist philosophy of harmony is expressed in the metaphysics of yin and yang. Yin is darkness. Yang is light. Together they form the T'ai Chi, or Great Ultimate. Yin and yang stand in bipolar relationship with one another, each one requiring the other for definition: without down, no up; without left, no right; without darkness, no light; without female, no male; without primary, no secondary, and so forth. This however does not entail duality, because the bipolar dynamic operates within a holistic context in which everything is inseparably interconnected with everything else. In Taoist metaphysics this insight is expressed as that the T'ai Chi originates from and is one with Wu Chi, whereas the Wu Chi is the Non-being ultimate, which is prior to and the source of all being, but which is in itself Non-being. Non-being does not mean nothingness in the literal sense, but no-thing-ness as in not anything in particular.

A misconception of yin/yang metaphysics is that yin and yang stand in relationship to one another as two sides of a balanced algebraic formula. It is not the case that yin and yang are of equal value. Yin is of greater value, for which yang is a secondary and augmentive value. Yin exists at two levels: first it is the Non-being that is prior and gives birth to being; and second is the relative non-being that stands alongside being in interdependent interaction with it. In the first sense, Non-being is absolute and prior to manifested existence. In the second sense, non-being exists within manifested relativity and is interdependent upon it. The two conditions of such are still related insofar as absolute Non-being enters into manifested relativity in order to produce being. Tao as Mother is that mode of Non-being producing the relative universe of being. Being as such has no existence apart from Non-being.

In biology there is what is known as parthenogenesis. Life comes from the female, and it is possible for life to self-generate from the female without the male. That is to say, all the bio-chemical components and mechanisms for regeneration of life exist within the female. The male acts as a stimulus to put the process in motion, and to contribute to genetic diversity. A male may be, in a manner of speaking, thought of as an incomplete female. In yin/yang metaphysics, yin is parthenogenic, but acts through yang (which she creates out of herself) to create diversity. From *Lao-tzu* we read:

3

"The way that can be talked about is not the constant Way.
The name that can be named is not the constant Name.
Non-being is the name of the origin of Heaven and Earth;
Being is the name of the mother of all things.
Therefore:
    Constantly in Non-being, one wishes to
    Contemplate its (the Way's) subtlety.
    Constantly in Being, one wishes to
    Contemplate its path.
These two come from the same source, but are different
in name.
The same source is called Mystery.
Mystery and more mystery,
It is the gateway to myriad subtleties." [2]

Mother is mother by way of having children—no children, no motherhood. Being expressed as T'ai-chi is the Mother of all things, but Non-being expressed as Wu-chi is the origin of Heaven and Earth. Both come from the same source, which is the mysterious Way, and the function of the Way is female. The function of the Way as female becomes Mother by way of the manifested Being. The Way is beyond naming. Things in manifested existence can be named, but the source of being—Non-being—is beyond names, and it is of the essence-less essence of the Way. More from *Lao-tzu:*

'The spirit of the valley never dies;
It is called the mysterious female.
The gate of the mysterious female
Is called the roots of Heaven and Earth.
Continuously it seems to exist.
There is no labor in its use." [3]

The first line refers to Non-being. The valley is an allegory to emptiness, whereas spirit is the function of emptiness. Such is the Mysterious Female, which is the root of the universe. Again, the Way

---

[2]   Wu, *The Book of Lao-tzu,* Chapter 1

[3]   Wu, *The Book of Lao-tzu,* Chapter 6

functions as the Mysterious Female. When she gives birth to Being, she becomes the Mother. The Chinese words that are translated as "metaphysics" can be more literally translated as "dark study." The word for "dark" is also used for "mystery." In Philosophical Taoism, truth is dark and mysterious. It may be said that there is wisdom in darkness that no light can see. This darkness is an attribute of the female. In contradiction to the monotheistic idea that god is a white male, in may be suggested by Taoism that God is a black women. In the mythological motifs of primal humanity the Great Goddess is dark like the night sky and the ground of fertile earth, and she encompasses a primal chaos, which is the dark watery womb, giving forth the abundance of life. The *Lao-tzu* again:

> "There was something formed in chaos;
> It existed before heaven and earth.
> Still and solitary,
> It alone stands without change.
> It is all-pervasive without being exhausted.
> It may be the mother of the world.
> I do not know its name, but name it the Way . . .
>
> The world has a beginning;
> It is the mother of the world.
> One can know the son,
> Having known the son
> One should stay with the mother."[4]

According to Yi Wu, professor of Chinese philosophy at the California Institute of Integral Studies, the mother/son relationship entails: root/end; substance/function; one/many; simplicity/complexity; spirit/[material]; non-action/action; wisdom/knowledge. He goes on to write, "To return to the mother is to return to the Way—to roots, substance, oneness, simplicity, non-action, and wisdom."[5] This is the meaning of having virtue.

---

4   Wu, *The Book of Lao-tzu, Chapters* 25 and 42
5   Wu, *The Book of Lao-tzu.* 189

The Chinese word for virtue is "te," which can also be translated as "power." When translated as power, it means something akin to the vitality of life, like that of a healthy organism or the healing properties of herbal medicine. An underlying notion here is that there is a fundamental relationship between morality and health. Indeed one may speak of immorality as a kind of sickness. Western ethical philosophy is often dichotomized in a duality of good versus evil. Much of the historical backdrop of this mode of thinking is Zoroastrianism, which influenced Jewish religion just prior to the emergence of Christianity. In the mythology of Zoroastrianism, and consequently in Christianity and Islam, evil became personified as the devil. In the mythological motifs of these religions we have a cosmic war in which one side must win, the good side, and evil must be destroyed at the end of history. Entailed in this mythos is a linear notion of time with an absolute beginning and an end.

Among indigenous people there is no devil, and time is associated with place in a pattern of eternal return in which life renews itself, and mythic beginnings are ever—present in each moment. The Taoist concept of virtue is derivative of indigenous philosophy, such that it is not a matter of good versus evil, but of the condition of health in contrast to the conditions of sickness. A healthy human being is not intentionally good, nor is a sick human intentionally bad. A person with a "good heart" who is whole and at one with his deeper nature in harmony with the Way is naturally good. In Chinese the word for "heart" is the same as for "mind," for that which thinks is also that which feels and the heart/mind is one and the same. The ethno-psychology implied in this concept differs greatly from that promulgated by the West, whereas in the West the mind is a function of the brain, in China the mind is a function of the vital life energy of the whole body, and is centered in the heart. Virtue as such is the condition of having a healthy heart/mind and body, whereas the body itself must be in accords with the Way of Great Harmony with Nature as a whole. In the words of *Lao-tzu:*

> "To keep the spirit and body embracing Oneness,
> can you let them not be separate?
> To concentrate the breath for attaining softness, can you
> be like an infant?

To wash and clear the mysterious vision, can you eliminate
all flaws?
To love the people and govern the state, can you be without
knowledge?
To open and close the Heavenly gates, can you be the female?
To understand all things in the four directions, can you be
in non-action?
To produce them and nourish them,
To produce without possessing,
To act without taking credit,
To [encourage] growth without controlling,
This is called mysterious virtue." [6]

In the first line is the issue of spirit and body. Virtue is the oneness
of these two. Separation or fragmentation of these is contrary to virtue.
In the second line the key term is "breath," which is a translation of
"ch'i" which is a term for omni-present life energy. It is viewed that
this bio-energy is the very stuff of the Universe. As one harmonizes
with ch'i and becomes one in heart/mind, one becomes one with
Nature, and this yields virtue. This relates to the state of the infant
insofar as one is born with virtue whole and complete. Separation
and fragmentation come later when one learns to behave contrary to
the Way. Knowledge is that which yields disharmony. By "knowledge"
what is meant is a mode of being in which psychic differentiates into
subject/object as to fragment them into a separation of ego from
the self as Deep Ecology, thus dividing the whole into artificial parts
negating the depth of wisdom of the Way. In Chapter Forty-eight of
Lao-tzu we read, "to pursue learning is to increase daily," whereas "to
practice the Way is to decrease daily," and this unto effortless action.
The nonaction of effortless action is to be, allegorically speaking, like
the female. The *Lao-tzu:*

"Knowing the male and keeping the female,
One will be the streambed of the world.
To be the streambed of the world,
One will not depart from the constant virtue

---

6   Wu, *The Book of Lao-tzu,* Chapter 10

But will return again to infancy.
Knowing the white and keeping to the black,
One will be the pattern of the world.
To be the pattern of the world,
One will not deviate from the constant virtue
But will return to the non-ultimate.
Knowing the honor and keeping to the mean,
One will be the valley of the world.
Being the valley of the world,
One's constant virtue is complete;
One returns to simplicity.
When the uncarved block is divided, it becomes vessels.
The sage uses it to become a leader.
Therefore, the great system will not cut apart." [7]

Virtue is innate. All that is required for it to manifest is the harmony of yin and yang—and this also is innate to life when nonaction is the norm. With nonaction one resides in the Great Ultimate (T'ai Chi), which is Non-Ultimate (Wu Chi). It is the Great Ultimate that is Non-Ultimate in that there is nothing beyond it. It is the uncarved block insofar that it is prior to things. It is the Great Harmony that exists within Nature. This Great Harmony is not made—it is discovered pre-existing within the groundless ground of being. Lao-tzu teaches that if one tries to take control over the world in an effort to improve it, one will only ruin it. The more one acts on the world, the more problems one creates. There is evidence of this in the techno-industrial age. From the paradigms of Francis Bacon and John Locke, the West is exerting an effort to subdue and improve the world. The result is the most destructive force in human history, threatening much of the life of our planet. The ecologists are now telling us that if we are to survive we must harmonize human activity with the norms of Nature. Philosophical Taoism agrees and goes on to assert that harmony comes out of the virtue of nonaction.

Pre-patriarchal Neolithic cultures are regarded in the Taoist view as societies that embody perfect virtue. These societies, which are the backdrop of later historical development, are of a matrilineal

---

[7]   Wu, The book of Lao-tzu, Chapter 28

gynocentric age. In the romantic imagination of the Chinese mythos this earlier age is associated with Shen Nung, the legendary founder of agriculture. In the Taoist writing of *Chuang-tzu,* it states that this age was one of peace in which people lived chose to Nature and were locally self-reliant. It was a time of perfect virtue in which they "knew their mothers but not their fathers"—in other words their culture was matrilineal. It was a time of uncarved simplicity in which people lived in accordance with their true nature. As Chinese civilization became imperialistic and oppressive, there arose in popular imagination the notion of a golden age of ancient utopia. This mythos became central to the political philosophy of Taoism, such as to call society back to Nature, back to the age of perfect virtue. This ideal is expressed in *Lao-tzu* thus:

> "There can be a small state with few people.
> Let it have many vessels; the people will not use them.
> Let the people value death and not move to far places.
> Though there are boats and carriages, there is no place to ride them.
> Though there are arm and weapons, there is no place to display them.
> Let the people again tie knots of rope [rather than use written language]
> and use them.
> Sweet their food, beautiful their clothes, peaceful their living, happy their customs.
> Neighboring states can see each other,
> The sounds of cocks and dogs can be heard by each other,
> But the people will grow old and die, never having visited each other." [8]

Anthropologist Levi Strauss suggested that culture has been in decline since the Neolithic. Gary Snyder, for his part, believes that culture was already in decline by the Neolithic, and that we need to go back to the Paleolithic to find humanity at her best! This position resembles Rousseau's theory of the "noble savage." Jean-Jacques

---

[8] Wu, *The Book of Lao-tzu,* Chapter 80

Rousseau argued that human life was at its best when humans lived in a "state-of-nature." Civilization is as such a mistake that robs humanity of her original freedom and enslaves humankind to the chains of civil society. Rousseau's position is the antithesis of Thomas Hobbes, who argued that life in a state-of-nature is a state-of-war, each person against the others. According to Hobbes, life in the war of the state-of-nature was "poor, nasty, brutish and short."

Civil society for Hobbes is thus a means of escaping the harshness and violence of the state-of-war in nature. Morality, it would follow, originates from something outside of human nature, and is superimposed on the person through social domestication. The underlying assumption is that human nature is bad, which is the dominant assumption with regard to human nature throughout most of the history of Western thought. It is this assumption that Rousseau called into question. Human life in a state-of-nature is good, he asserted, and human nature is good. The noble savage does not require moral conditioning in order to be good—he is good by the fact of being amoral, that is to say, by not having moral conditioning superimposed on his original nature. It is civilized humanity, those who have been conditioned and domesticated into concepts of morality who becomes violent, greedy, hateful, and so forth. It is the social, and not the natural, that is the cause of the problem. The preponderance of evidence supports a Rousseauian view on this point. For most of the history of human existence, humanity lived in hunting-and-gathering tribes. Such a way of life is a state-of-nature. A prime example of hunting and gathering culture living in a state-of-nature is the Pygmies of the Congo. Colin Turnbull, an anthropologist who studied these people first hand over many years, wrote this about them:

"There were no chiefs, no formal councils. In each aspect of Pygmy life there might be one or two men or women who were more prominent than others, but usually for good practical reasons. This showed up most clearly of all in the settling of disputes. There was no judge, no jury, no courts . . . If you ask a Pygmy why his people have no chiefs, no lawgivers, no councils, or no leaders, he will answer with misleading simplicity, 'Because we are the people of the forest.' The forest, the great provider, is the one standard by which all deeds and thoughts are judged; it is the chief, the lawgiver, the leader, and the final arbitrator." [9]

What Turnbull says of the Pygmies would apply equally as well as a description of most hunting-and-gathering cultures. Moreover, the fundamental values, that make these primal cultures workable, extend into Neolithic societies. Sharing and caring is what holds these cultures together into an integral whole. In contradistinction, patriarchal civilizations are based on force and violence. Civil order depends on violence and threat of violence. The army and the police force are the backbone of civil society. The claim of the system is that human nature cannot be trusted, and that people will not behave well toward one another if they are free of the limits imposed by the incentives of punishments and rewards. This claim is falsified by the fact that cultures exist in which sharing and caring are axiomatic to the social dynamic without the threat of violence. Interpersonal harmony and harmony with Nature are the standards that ground these societies into a healthy working whole. Among American Indians this philosophy is known as the Medicine Wheel. The Iroquois refer to it as the "original instruction," which is the teaching of "Great Harmony," which comes from the "Great Mystery." From a message to the Western world from the Haudenosauness (Iroquois) one reads:

"The original instruction directs that we who walk about on the Earth are to express a great respect, an affection, and a gratitude toward all the spirits which create and support Life. We give a greeting and thanksgiving to the many supporters of our own lives—the corn, beans, squash, the wind, the sun. When people cease to respect and express gratitude for these many things, then all life will be destroyed, and human life on this planet will come to an end . . .

"We have seen that not all people of the Earth show the same kind of respect for this world and its being. The Indo-European people who have colonized our lands have shown very little respect for the things that create and support Life . . .

"The Western culture has been horribly exploitative and destructive of the Natural World. Over 140 species of birds and animals were utterly destroyed since the European arrival in the Americas, largely

---

[9]   Turnbull, *The Forest People*. 110

because they were unusable in the eyes of the invaders. The forests were leveled, the water polluted, the Natives subjected to genocide. The vast herds of herbivores were reduced to mere handfuls; the buffalo nearly became extinct. Western technology and the people who have employed it have been the most amazingly destructive force in all of human history. No natural disaster has ever destroyed as much. Not even the Ice Age counted as many victims . . .

"Today the species of Man is facing a question of the very survival of the species. The way of life known as Western Civilization is on a death path on which their own culture has no viable answers. When faced with the reality of their own destructiveness, they can only go forward into areas of more efficient destruction . . .

"The air is foul, the water poisoned, the trees dying, the animals are disappearing. We think even the systems of weather are changing. Our ancient teaching warned us that if Man interfered with the Natural laws, these things would come to be. When the last of the Natural Way of Life is gone, all hope for human survival will be gone with it. And our Way of life is fast disappearing, a victim of the destructive processes." [10]

Environmental conservationist Raymond Dasmann makes a distinction between what he calls "ecosystem-based cultures" and "biosphere cultures." The former are indigenous cultures that live in harmony with the natural environment. The latter are cultures that exploit the natural environment. The Roman Empire was of the latter kind, which, writes Gary Snyder, "would strip whole provinces for the benefit of the capital, and villa-owing Roman aristocrats would have huge slave-operated farms in the south using giant wheeled plows. Southern Italy never recovered."[11]

The multi-national corporations of today with their techno-industrial exploitation of biosphere Earth also belong to the latter kind. Biospherical cultures are hierarchical and authoritarian, with centralized power and programming. They use large concentrations of wealth to manipulate markets and people for profit and power, which exploits bio-systems and their inhabits for what they may gain, then to move on to other bio-systems to repeat the process—in a word, they are destroyers of life. The biospherical

---

[10]   Akwesasne, *Basic Call to Consciousness.* 71-78

[11]   Snyder, *The Old Ways.* 60-61

cultures are pathological outgrowth of patriarchal sociopolitics. Gynocentric cultures are ecosystem based.

Pre-patriarchal times were benevolent anarchy; government and economic systems did not interfere with the natural goodness of the people, therefore people were naturally good. With patriarchal bioshperical centralized authoritarian sociopolitics, normality turns to abnormality. The Natural Way as a normative element of a healthy society is parted with, and society becomes pathological. The archaeological evidence presented by University of California Professor Marija Gimbutas and corroborated by other professionals in the field, clearly reveals that Neolithic humanity lived in villages along waterways with little to no fortification or evidence of much in the way of weaponry, but then came the patriarchal warlords spreading across the land. This forced villages to move into the highlands and build fortifications. Thus the arms race began.

The biospheical cultures, in their greed for profit, transformed the world into a place of force and violence. Lao-tzu asserted that the essence of his teaching is that to live a violent life is to die an unnatural death. Harmony with the Way of Nature is to live at peace. The way of war is contrary to this. The sociopolitical element of Lao-tzu's teaching is to suggest a normative perspective in which a healthy society may be understood. With the Natural Way comes virtue, and with virtue comes a manner of living based on natural goodness and ecological wisdom. This wisdom is embodied in the image of the Circle of Life or the Medicine Wheel, which is the symbol of the original instructions. Patriarchal civilization is built on a philosophy of the broken Circle, which results in the ecology crisis. In order to survive we must heal our broken ways and return to the wholeness of the Circle of Life. This point is elegantly stated in the words of ecologist Barry Commoner:

"Human beings have broken out of the circle of life, driven not by biological need, but by the social organization which they have devised to 'conquer' nature: means of gaining wealth that are governed by requirements conflicting with those which govern nature. The end result is the environmental crisis, a crisis of survival. Once more, to survive, we must close the circle . . ." [12]

---

[12]   Barry Commoner, *The Closing Circle*. 298-299

THE WAY OF THE SOUTH: SACRED HOOP

The aboriginal worldview reflects the wisdom of the Way as may be seen in the philosophy of the Medicine Wheel, which teaches that the world mirrors the conditions of one's own being. It is said that as one believes, so one sees. We edit with our beliefs such that we see what we want to see and disregard the rest. The world reflects what one is such that one sees only that which is in oneself. There is in Western thought the notion of an external Universe, but not so in aboriginal worldviews. There is the Natural world that we are all part of, and much of it is outside of one's personal experience, but it is not external to the totality of one's being; rather the Natural world is the essence of one's being. It belongs to oneself. It is oneself. Furthermore, it reflects self, whereas everything one experiences is a teaching. All of life is a Circle that forms the Sacred Hoop, which connect everything to everything. A circle symbolizes the world and oneself. This is the basis for the philosophy of the Medicine Wheel. The Sioux medicine-man Black Elk speaks of the Circle thus:

"You have noticed that everything an Indian does is in a circle, and that is because the Power of the World always works in circles, and everything tries to be round. In the old days when we were a strong and happy people, all our power came to us from the sacred hoop of the nation, and so long as the hoop was unbroken, the people flourished. The flowering tree was the living center of the hoop, and the circle of the four quarters nourished it. The east gave peace and light, the south gave warmth, the west gave rain, and the north with its cold and mighty wind gave strength and endurance. This knowledge came to us from the outer world with our religion. Everything the Power of the World does it does in a circle. The sky is round, and I have heard that the earth is round like a ball, and so are the stars.

The wind, in its greatest power whirls. Birds make their nest in circles for theirs is the same religion as ours. The sun comes forth and goes down again in a circle. The moon does the same, and both are round. Even the seasons form a great circle in their changing, and always come back again to where they were. The life of a man is a circle from childhood to childhood, and so it is in everything where power moves. Our tepees were round like the nests of birds, and these were always set in a circle, the nation's hoop, a nest of many nests where the Great Spirit meant for us to hatch our children." [1]

The Tai Chi forms the circle with its yin and yang. The circle itself is the symbol of the Tao. In Native American thought this is call the "Great Mystery." It is so called because it is understood that the supreme ultimate reality is beyond the finite capacities of the mind to understand. One may ask the question "why" forever. There is no ultimate answer. The question, "Why is there existence?" is what American Indian philosophy answers with "Great Mystery." It just is, and one lives it, and apart from the wisdom of living life there is no comprehension. Like the Tao it cannot be understood with words.

As I mentioned in the Introduction to this book, the Medicine Wheel is divided into the four cardinal directions, each direction symbolizing a mode of being. Each mode is associated with a season and a phase in life. The East belongs to Spring, which is the place of birth. The South belongs to Summer, which is the place of childhood. The West belongs to Fall, which is the place of adulthood. The North belongs to Winter, which is the place of old age and death (the Great-Give-Away).

A newborn first learns through sensing. The East is the place of learning by entering into the world of sensory experience. In psychological development, emotions are primary to thought. A child learns to feel before she or he learns to think. The South as the place of childhood is also the place of family, which is held together with love. It is the summer place, with its warmth. In many American Indian cultures the transition from childhood to adulthood is marked by the Vision Quest. It is through Vision that one discovers the spiritual bases of life. Vision and spiritual consciousness come through the power of intuition. This is found in the West of the Wheel. And then to the

---

[1]   Neihart, *Black Elk Speaks.* 164-165

North is the place of knowledge, which is an outcome of accumulated experience. Knowledge depends on memory, and also on cultural traditions.

Culture shapes the way we think. Indian thinking is very different from that of Westerners. Western thinking is analytic, whereas Indian thinking is more holistic. A holistic way of thought integrates the accumulated experience of life into a relationship with tribal ways. The elders are responsible for the education of the youth and for the spiritual guidance of the people. The Great-Give-Away is to take the wisdom of age and give it to the people. In this way, death is rebirth as the wisdom of the ancestors is renewed with each generation.

Central to the Medicine Wheel is the teaching of Great Harmony. This teaches that to be whole, and thus healthy, requires an integration of the four modes into a harmony. Each mode is augmented by the others in the process of self-actualization. One may think of this in terms of Maslow's "hierarchy of needs," which asserts that basic needs like food and water must be accommodated before one may go on to higher needs like art and music. The idea of hierarchy is somewhat alien to most Indian tribes and inconsistent with the metaphysics of the Medicine Wheel, so one may instead think of the circle of needs. The East is like Maslow's physical needs. The South is the place of emotional needs. The West and North go with the so-called "higher" needs. Maslow asserts that if needs are not fulfilled the result is psychological deficiency, which in turn yields psychological illness. With both the Medicine Wheel philosophy and the Humanistic Psychology of Maslow, when needs are fulfilled in ongoing growth, then self-actualization comes about.

Carl Jung paired thinking with feelings, and sensing with intuition, which is consistent with the Medicine Wheel. In representing the Wheel one draws a line through a circle connecting North to South, and another at right angles connecting East with West, thus producing a cross inside of a circle. The point of intersection of the lines in the center of the circle symbolizes Great Harmony. The relationship of say, North to South, is such that if one places a priority on one, say the North, then the other becomes an anti-priority, in this case the South. In other words, if thinking becomes a priority, then feeling becomes an anti-priority. It was in terms of this understanding that some Indians referred to the Europeans as the Winter-way people. By this it is meant that the Europeans are North-like in hyper-thought, with the result of being emotionally cold. The priority of thinking created a deficiency in feeling. In Indian country there are shamans who refer to Anglos as "emotionally retarded." For an Anglo-American to become healthy through the Medicine of the Wheel, the thawing warmth of the South is needed—that is to say, thinking harmonized with feeling.

Taoist metaphysics applied to the Medicine Wheel works this way: thinking is the yang to feeling as yin; and sensing is yang to intuition as yin. According to Jungian psychology, sensing and intuition go together as modes of perception; and thinking and feeling go together as mode of judgment. Perception is yin to judgment as yang. There is also extraversion, which is associated in primal mythos with the sky, which is yang; and there is introversion, belonging to earth as yin. Great Harmony requires balance of yin and yang, which entails balance of thinking with feeling, sensing with intuition, and so forth.

The Medicine Wheel teaches that each of us is born with a gift, which is the place on the Wheel that is what we are most predisposed to in our growth into integration with the whole. In Jungian theory it is said that of the four modes of consciousness, one will be a preferred orientation. If one has preference for a judgment orientation, then one will have a preference for either thinking or feeling; and if one's orientation is for perception, then one will have preference for either intuition or sensing. There are thus four basic personality types.

In addition there is also the manner in which a person relates to the world, either as an extrovert, in which case the gift is outwardly displayed, or introvert, in which case the person's inner life is the domain of the gift. If a person is a feeling type, then either intuition or sensation will be auxiliary. If this person is an introvert, then the inner world of feeling will be the gift, and the outer diameter will be either intuition or sensation depending on which auxiliary mode is preferred.

Suppose that an introverted feeling type has intuition as her or his auxiliary preference, then being attentive to the world of sensing would not come easy, and clear thinking would be even more difficult. If a person is an extraverted thinking type, then he or she would have difficulty relating to feelings. Jung gives us the concept of the shadow, which references that part of our psyche that we have little to no direct awareness of but which shapes some of our personality. For a thinking type, feelings reside within the shadow.

Each gift comes with its own set of difficulties, and learning from those difficulties becomes a source of growth in one's life. Each person must begin with and rely on her or his natural gift, for to do otherwise would be self-denial. Hence, the Medicine Wheel teaches to learn with one's gift by entering into relationships with others. What one cannot easily enter into on one's own, one may within relationships with others. The Medicine Wheel teaches that every person one encounters, indeed everything, is a Medicine Wheel of oneself. That which one is, one sees. Accordingly the feeling intuitive person may learn of sensing and thinking by being in relationship with sensing types and thinking types, or confronting situations that call forth these modes. Always, however, one must remain true to one's own gift.

Western psychology places a great deal of importance on atomistic individuality. For this reason Westerners seem to feel that they must be self-complete. Perhaps that is why loneliness is so common in Western civilization. Aboriginal ethos is quite different on this point. No one may be complete unto oneself. It is only by being in relationships with others that one may be whole. The indigenous sense of self is inseparable from the environment, and this means both the social and the ecological together. Aboriginal ethno-identity is much like a personal gestalt that is incomplete apart from relationships. Indeed among American Indians one prays for the benefit of "all my relations" who include those with four legs, and those with wings, and the bugs, and also the rocks and tress and all of the plants and everything that is within the web of life. Self-actualization is thus not so much a question of personal growth as it is growth of people within culture. The Vision Quest, which in many tribes is solitary but for the preparation and aftermath, has it meaning within a matrix of cultural understanding. It is designed to attune one to one's natural gift, but the gift, which is personal, is incomplete until it is used in relationship with others.

The philosophy of Great Harmony exists at three levels: the personal, the social, and the environmental. These three are inseparable. Personal harmony is brought about when the modes of being within oneself are in harmony, but this can only come about in relation with the social. Social harmony is brought about when the people harmonize with each other, but this can only come about when the society is in harmony with Nature. The supreme reality of Nature is the Great Mystery. Harmony with the Great Mystery is balance, which in Taoism is said to be between yin and yang. In Jungian terms it is the balance of introversion and extroversion. In archetypal language expressed in mytho-poetic imagery this is the point of balance of Earth and Sky. In both American Indian and Chinese philosophy harmony with the Way is the balance of Earth and Sky. In Chinese thought the Sky is yang and the Earth is yin, whereas American Indians call the Earth Mother, and the Sky Father. Sky is outwardness and hence goes with extraversion. Earth is inwardness, like the image of a cave, and hence belongs to introversion. The harmony of the modes of consciousness depends on balance of male and female.

The Great Mystery or Tao is the nameless groundless ground of the Universe. It is the foundationless foundation of existence. The Tao is the origins and underlying suchness of the world. In *Lao-tzu* we read:

> "The Way brings forth one,
> One brings forth two,
> Two brings forth three,
> Three bring forth all things.
> All things carry the dark [yin] and embrace the light [yang],
> And make them harmonize with empty energy [ch'i]." [2]

To say that the Way brings forth the One is to say that the Way is prior to the One, and therefore not the One. The Way is empty, like zero. The Way as emptiness is the womb out of which everything is born. Everything is related to the Way as Mother, and so is One. Lao-tzu goes on to assert that the One gives birth to the Two, and the Two gives birth to the Three. Whenever one has something, then that something is such in relation to something else. In order to be cognitive of phenomena there must be figure and ground. One always perceives the world in terms of gestalts where "this" has this-ness because there is "that" with that-ness; and that-ness is such because

---

[2]   Wu, *The book of Lao-tzu*, Chapter 42

of this-ness. Thus it is that they co-arise as three: this and that and the relation between this and that.

The two primal energies of the universe are yin and yang. These energies are ultimately one, and of the essence of empty ch'i. This ch'i is omni-present synergetic energy. It is not energy as understood by classical physics. It is a non-physical energy that is within the synergy of relationships. Nothing exists apart from relational vectors that connect everything to everything else. Things in relationship do not produce the vectors relationships; rather the things themselves are produced by the synergy of relationship. The whole is greater than the sum of the parts and the parts are produced by the whole. Ch'i is synergy. The intensification of ch'i gives birth to life; the intensification of the ch'i of life gives birth to awareness; and further intensification yields insight, which is to have Vision of the empty ground of being or Great Mystery.

Everything is always changing. This is axiomatic to the philosophy of the *I-Ching (Book of Changes)*. The *I-Ching* describes the nature of changes and so explicates the principles that govern the evolution of changes. The relational dynamics of yin and yang are fundamental, and fundamental to this is the principle of reversion which states that given any movement or state of being taken to the extreme will transform into its opposite. For examples: the sun at its zenith begins its descent; the coldest time of winter begins the movement toward summer; the assertion of the greatest strength is followed by weakness; and so forth. Yin/yang dynamics are most fundamental to the principle of reversion. Extreme yang turns into yin; extreme yin turns into yang.

The *I-Ching* symbolizes yang with a sold line and yin with a broken line. With this we have a binary code of either a positive vector (sold line) or a negative vector (broken line). The negative here means quiescence or no activity. Yang is activity. The interaction of yin and yang are symbolized as bigrams, there being four: yang in terms of itself, yin in term of itself, yang in relation to yin, and yin in relation to yang. This gives the four fold symmetry which is expressed in the four directions: South being yang of yang, North being yin of yin, East being the yang of yin, and West being the yin of yang. The Chinese system is different from the Native American Wheel that has the North as thinking which is yang, and South as feeling which is yin. This difference is due to the difference of discourse whereas the American Indian Wheel is about the internal state of the psyche and the Chinese is about the outer world of the environment. Summer is hot, which is a kind of activity and thus yang. The psyche to balance itself from the environmental yang gravitates to yin as feeling. Winter is yin, so the psyche balances itself with the yang of thinking.

When one adds to the Wheel 'up' and 'down' then there is a triangulation effect. To visualize this imagine a circle with the four directions and the axis running up and down from the center. The up is yang and the down is yin. Now imagine a line running out from the center to the East, and another line running up at an angle from the East to connect with the line up from the center, and there is a triangle. There are four such triangles running up, and four more going down, with a total of eight, which correlates with the eight trigams of the *I-Ching*. One may think of these trigams as triangles in which each line or vector has a value of 1 or 0, yes or no, on or off. According to Buckminster Fuller, the triangle is the most basic structure in the universe. In order to have system dynamics, structures need to be related to other structures, and so the most basic system is between two triangles, the most efficient arrangement of which is a tetrahedron, which consists of six vectors. With binary vector dynamics this gives sixty-four possibilities, which is symbolized in the *I-Ching* as the hexagrams. It is the arrangement of these sixty-four hexagrams that forms the textual outline of the *I-Ching*.

The first hexagram of the *I-Ching* is called "Creative Heaven," which is composed of all yang lines. The next is called the "Receptive Earth" with all yin lines. In both Chinese and American Indian cosmologies it is said that the world was created by the relationship of Earth and Sky. The relationship of Earth and Sky is the axis of the Medicine Wheel. The four directional Powers depends on these two Primal Powers. These Powers cannot stand independently of one another, and are continually transforming one another. In this process conditions are continuously losing equilibrium and then recovering it. Yin and yang are by nature seeking to balance each other. The last hexagram in the traditional sequence is called "After Completion" which is composed of an equal number of alternating yang and yin lines. This reflects the ideal of homeostasis that is a virtual state that cannot long stand in a universe of omni-changes.

On the Pythagorean table of opposites things are always opposed: right versus left, light versus dark, good versus evil, and so forth. This may seem similar to the philosophy of the *I-Ching*, but for one major difference—for Pythagoras and those who follow his line of thought there exists a dualism in terms of which the right and good are superior and must win by conquest or even destruction of the left, and the bad. For the ancient Greeks the world was a tragic place with much suffering, and it was a war-based culture focused on conquest and domination. This is far removed from Taoism and the aboriginal roots thereof which proclaim the world of Nature as good and a source of joy, and that goodness is found within the harmony of opposites. From this aboriginal point of view the philosophy of the Greeks is one of disharmony and disease!

The philosophy of the Greeks finds its origins in the patriarchal conquest of gynocentric cultures. It entails a dualism of sky against earth—a way of death spread across the world with the war chariot. Plato in the *Phaedrus* uses the image of the chariot as a metaphor for teaching the Pythagorean dualism. He divides the psyche into three parts symbolized as two horses and a charioteer. We have one horse to the left and the other to the right. The left is dark and bad; the right is white and good. In addition there is the context set wherein the earth is bad and the sky is good. Moreover bodily passion is associated with the earth and thus bad, but disembodied reason is associated with the sky and therefore good. And thus the aim is to disembody and fly into the sky leaving behind all that is bad.

"At last they [charioteer and the right-hand horse] pass out of the body, unwaged, but eager to soar, and thus obtain no mean reward of love and madness. For those who have once begun the heavenward pilgrimage may not go down again to darkness and journey beneath the earth, but they live in light always; happy companions in their pilgrimage . . . Whereas the attachment of the non-lover [the dark horse], which is alloyed with a worldly prudence and has worldly and niggardly ways of doling out benefits, will bread in your soul those vulgar qualities which the populace applaud, will send you bowling round the earth during a period of nine thousand years, and leave you a fool in the world below." [3]

---

[3]   Wilbur and Allen, *The Worlds of Plato and Aristotle*. 38-41.

In the United States two cars arrive at a four-way stop at the same time. By the rule of the road, the car to the right has the right-of-way. The right rules! Historical progress in Western civilization is symbolized by a line moving from left to right. The reader is reading this from left to right. Most people write with their right hand. The root meaning of "sinister" is "on the left." Economic progress is graphed by a line that moves up and to the right. In analytic geometry the upper right hand quadrant is assigned the value of positive/ positive. Down and to the left is negative/ negative. On a map, north is up and east is right. In most of the major older cities in Western civilization, e.g. London, Paris, New York, etc. the greatest concentration of wealth tends to be in the northeast, whereas city dumps, sewage treatment plants, polluting industries and the like tend to be in the southwest.

In the last Book of Plato's *Republic*, is the myth of Ur, in which a man has an encounter with death, but is allowed to come back to life to tell of his experience. He reports having seen four gateways: one being up and to the right, another down and to the left, the others being up and to the left, and down and to the right. Good souls went through the gateway that was up and to the right for their heavenly reward. Bad souls went down and to the left for punishment in hell. After bad souls had received their allotted punishment, they were permitted to reincarnate by way of the gateway down and to the right—by moving right they redeemed themselves. Good souls not good enough to stay in heaven reincarnated through the up and to the left gateway—to move left is to fall from heaven.

The neuro-somatic or kinesthetic sensation of up and to the right is synchronistic to the upper left part of the brain. This part of the brain is believed to be the physical locus of thinking in most right-handed people. The right hemisphere of the brain, which is synchronistic to the left side of the body, is said to be the locus of intuition and feeling. Putting this in terms of Taoist metaphysics, left-brain is yang, right brain is yin, cerebral is yang and the limbic is yin. Using the bigrams of the *I-Ching* one may define the four most basic relations of yin and yang in relation to the nature of the four modes of consciousness in reference to the above stated assertion of the yin/yang structure of the brain thus: thinking, which belongs to the left cerebral, is yang /yang; feeling, which is right limbic, is yin /

yin; intuition, which is right cerebral, is yin of yang; sensation, which is left limbic, is yang of yin.

According to this understanding, the up-and-to-the-right orientation of Western civilization reflects its priority for yang and anti-priority for yin. This is further reflected in the central role that reason plays in Western philosophy—and reflected moreover in its get-ahead mentality. In Plato's philosophy of the divided line, there is division between that which is rational—which is placed above the line—and that that is irrational—which is placed below the line. Then he gives us the ascending line, which is an up-and-to-the-right movement from below to above. Plato divides the soul into three parts: the rational, the spirited, and the passions. In the above quote from *Phaedrus*, the rational belongs to the charioteer, the spirited belongs to the good horse, and the passions belong to the bad horse. By spirited Plato seems to mean attributes of the sensing types. By passion he appears to mean the yin-like attributes of feeling and intuition. Plato asserts that reason ought to rule and the others parts must obey. Sensing on its own for its own sake is not to be trusted, for apart from reason it may lead a person to passion. Some forms of intuition may be allowed if they serve the end of reason. The deeper forms of intuition, which are more akin to feeling, are not to be trusted. The passions associated with feeling are incapable of perfect submission to reason, thus the perfect condition in Plato's philosophy would be freedom from such passions.

On the Medicine Wheel the North is thinking and the East is sensation. The up-and-to-the-right-ism of the Northeast is the alliance of thinking with sensation. The Southwest for Plato is the place of hell. This is the feeling space of the passions. With Platonism there can be no harmony of the Northeast with the Southwest. In the American Indian philosophy of Great Harmony, the four modes must be in harmony in order for there to be health. From this point of view what Plato articulates is a philosophy of sickness. It is the foundational philosophy of Western Civilization.

Sigmund Freud divided the psyche into three parts: superego, ego, and id. These correspond with Plato: superego is reason, ego is spirited, and passion is id. In Freudian psychology neurosis is thought of as a condition of repression. That which is repressed is the libido which has its source within the id. Both Freud and Plato asserted that passion is the source of what is bad. Augustine, Luther, and many other theologians have asserted much the same view. Inborn human nature, they have said, is a product of sin and therefore is evil. What we have with such a view is more than just a priority placed upon reason, but also a negative judgment placed upon modes that fall beyond the control and comprehension of reason. On the Medicine Wheel the equivalent of sickness is a state of disharmony between the modes. Western ethos set up just such a disharmony by placing a strong negative judgment against passion.

According to what one may infer from Taoist metaphysics, civilizations suffer from too much yang and too little yin. Moreover, especially in the West and Middle East, there exists a hyper-yang repression of yin. The history of civilizations begins with the patriarchal overthrow of yin grounded cultures. Earth Goddess religions preceded Father Sky religions. Aboriginal understanding sees the world as a living being and thus created as through birth, which entails that the creator is Mother.

Although one's gender does not determine one's orientation, still I feel that Jung is justified in associating introversion with femininity, thus yin, and extraversion to masculinity, thus yang. In terms of the archetypal structure of the collective unconscious, this seems to work. I have already made reference to the mytho-poetic imagery of Mother Earth and Father Sky—that Earth is inwardness, and Sky is outwardness. Add to this that the power of female creativity is rooted in the power of organic growth. Growth is something that comes from within. Yang or male creativity is artificial like construction, which is outward-going activity. In the earliest of human societies, in hunting-and-gathering cultures, the women were the main providers of food, because of their attentiveness to plant life. They stayed close to home and close to organic patterns of growth. The men were the hunters, out-going for game. As far as one can generalize about collective gender behavior, men tend to be more extraverted, and women more introverted.

Jung writes of anima (femaleness within a male) and animus (maleness within a female). This notion is expressed in the symbol for yin and yang—a circle divided by an 'S' shaped-line into black and white with a white dot in the black and a black dot in the white. All humans have both maleness and femaleness within their makeup.

Among many indigenous tribes there is a belief that some people have maleness and femaleness equally. My Cherokee ancestors called such persons "s-gi-gi," which means one who has two genders in one body. The Samoans called such persons with male genitals "faafafine." When I lived in Samoa I had faafafine friends. On one occasion two of them were trying to sexually seduce me. I was politely declining the offer and suggesting to them that if they wanted sexual gratification then perhaps they might want to have sex with each other, to which one said in agreement with the other, "We cannot do that. We are not lesbians." Apparently sex with someone of the same gender is regarded as homosexual, but not between genders, whereas faafafine seen as a third gender goes beyond the binary logic of a two gender-system. Prior to going to Samoa I had been living with the Navajo who recognize four genders—men, women, feminine males and masculine females. This is common among many Indian cultures and other tribal people the world over. In some cultures there are even more genders. Most common is a third gender like faafafine that describes males with femininity. The prefix "faa" means "way" and "fafine" means "woman," thus "woman-way." I learned from the Samoans that for them there is no need for masculine women to have a separate gender category because a woman can be anything she wants and still be woman. In the primal cosmology of the Great Goddess the whole universe is female—it is all an expression of the Mother giving birth to herself. Maleness is a localized subset of femaleness that the Great Goddess creates out of the fabric of her own nature.

Contemporary American Indians refer to transgender people as "two spirits." By using the term "transgender" I mean people who do not fit within the binary of male/female, but embody both together. The two spirits are male and female as found in biological nature, and are akin to yin and yang. But yin and yang are not stagnant—they are in constant dynamic interplay in which they flow into each other transforming as they go. Because we have nouns in our language we tend to imagine that things thus named have fixed natures and we ascribe substance to them. Gender belongs to the domain of language and as such is a social construct. If this is not understood then social conventions can become tyrannical. This said it is useful to remember that there is a trans-linguistic biology such that long before there was culturally defined gender there was sexual activity. The evolution of sex is deeper than the cultural artifact of gender. Biology is an endless dance of change. The Navajo language reflects this better than most in having few nouns and mostly verbs.

In thinking about the psychological temperaments of environmental orientation in reference to anima and animus, I submit for consideration that the introverted male more easily harmonizes with his anima than does the extraverted male. And likewise the extraverted female more easily harmonize with her animus than does an introverted female. This follows from the same principle that a sensing type finds intuition difficult to understand, and the same for any type with regard to her or his opposite mode. What is true for the person, in this case, is true for the society as a whole—whereas the priority of extraversion in Western civilization has made it difficult for Westerners to understand introverted female nature.

Western societies have throughout history been racist, sexist, and homophobic. This once again comes down to the hyper-yang repression of yin. In racism the white race asserts itself as superior to darker-skinned people. The black race was regarded as the most inferior. We often hear about the 'light of reason' and father god as being in white light. Discovering truth is called "enlightenment" and ignorance is living in the dark. Rationalism gives us the light of logic, and empiricism gives us the light of experience—together they give us the light of science. What is down-and-to-the-left is excluded. Feelings and deep intuition are dark, fuzzy, imprecise, immeasurable, and so forth. The scientist does not trust the dark. In many of the high-culture religions darkness is associated with evil, and down with hell. All this is projected onto dark-skinned people. Much of the same is projected onto women. For centuries the power of women has been feared by phallocentric men, for women have a capacity that men do not and yet are dependent on, the power of reproduction! Women for the most part also have greater attunement to dark knowledge—deep intuition and feelings. The yin power is at home in the right side of the brain, which connects the psyche to that which Western humanity seems to most fear. This neurosis leads to homophobia. Women, according to early Christianity, are gateways of Satan. For a man to become as a woman is to invite Satan into his soul. It is to fall down-and-to-the-left, to enter into the anima. Thus the Western man is conditioned to fear homosexual feelings. Women as external phenomena are less threatening than internal feelings, for the patriarchal state has degraded women to the status of human cattle and thus made them controllable. But homosexual feeling are inside, and if felt imply loss of control, which in turn invites evil.

The Western world creates the very evil that it fears by setting up conditions that create disharmony. The priority of up-and-to-the right thinking (North) enslaved sensations (East), and yang/ Sky (extraversion), in conjunction with the repression of the down-and-to-the-left feelings (South), intuition (West), and yin/ Earth (introversion), yields disharmony. The cure consists of harmony of thinking with feelings, and sensation with intuition. This ultimately rests in the harmony of yang and yin in a kind of alchemical marriage.

In aboriginal understanding femininity is prior to masculinity. The notion of balance of yin and yang does not mean equality of function; rather it means that each relates to the other according to its appropriate nature; one does not dominate the other and each follows that which is transcendent to both yet inclusive of all—the Way. The nature of yang is extroverted activity. The nature of yin is introverted space. The point of balance in which the two harmonize is in effortless action in accords with the Way. The Way is transcendent to both yin and yang, yet it embraces both in and through Nature. The natural is that which is so of her-self. Nature acts, but not through effort. The nonactive is the natural ground for the active; hence yin is prior to yang.

Civilization is about making effort, about being ambitious, competitive, fighting to win, getting-ahead, and attempting to improve upon nature. The modern life style is "do doing never rest until the better is best," which in turn leads to "live fast and die young." In hyper-activity Western humanity developed an industrial complex in which life is enslaved to a materialistic cycle of producing and consuming. This life-style disrupts balance with Nature, yielding pathological conditions. Under these conditions the psyche feels dis-ease, a sense of incompleteness. This circumstance removes the psyche from that which gives to her a natural feeling of fullness and replaces it with the propaganda that economic activity will lead to the means unto fulfillment. This further blocks the psyche from fullness of Nature. Fulfillment does not come from the pleasures of gratifying artificially generated desires, indeed such desires are the roots of suffering. The 'evil' passions of Platonic thought are created by the patriarchal "reason" that oppresses/represses Nature. To heal this pathology requires in-tune-ment to the tranquility and joy of the Way, which for modern people requires embracing yin stillness. So long as Westernized humanity lacks this wisdom, it will continue to disrupt and destroy the ecology of our planet.

THE WAY OF THE WEST: COMING OF AGE

Alfred North Whitehead has suggested that the history of Western philosophy is a series of footnotes to Plato. What Whitehead essentially seems to mean by this is that Plato put forth the fundamental discourse of Western thought, and that Western philosophers have ever since operated within that discourse, employing the core assumptions entailed therein. The fact that Western philosophy operates within a preset frame of reference is not as important as what motivation underlies this process. In Plato is the basic ethno-psychological character of Western thought. From that ancient time until today, the essential ethos of the West has altered very little. The implications are that there is a psychological disposition that civilization historically perpetuates, and the principle means through which this occurs is cultural indoctrination. Most of this happens as unconscious imprinting. With this imprinting we inherit a mind-set without conscious knowledge of it as such. Subliminal cultural imprinting shapes our minds and the emotional undercurrent thereof. In terms of both personal development and cultural history what is imprinted earliest tends to be most powerful in shaping the predispositions of the mind and its overall structure. What is ancient is deeply ingrained in our minds and shapes our current states of being. Plato's skillful rhetoric, coupled with his position in history, gives a window into the ancient imprint of Western ethos. Moreover, Plato's views have been imprinted into history and therefore have contributed to the shaping of the Western ethos.

Sigmund Freud put forth the notion that civilization is essentially neurotic; or more precisely, civilization has the effect of making its members neurotic. Being neurotic means being repressed in such a means and manner as to be mostly if not altogether unconscious of the repression. More often than not, those who suffer from neuroses take said condition to be the normal state of the psyche. Under such repression the natural state of being is altered to make way for the domesticated state. Moreover, the natural state is denied (repressed) and pushed out of conscious life, resulting in the formation of the repressed unconscious. We are born with the id; the ego and superego are cultural artifacts. These artifacts are the fragmentation of consciousness generated by the psychodynamics of repression. This is seen in Plato's dividing line, which separates out the so-called "higher" from the "lower." The lower realm is associated with change and illusion, whereas the higher is the domain of what is assumed to be unchanging reality. The lower is equated with evil, whereas the higher is thought of as good. We are born into the lower, but through right education must be made to subdue what we are born with in favor of the higher. This sublimation is symbolized as the ascending line. It reflects the duality of Western ethos between mind and matter, spirit and flesh, culture and nature, man and women, and so forth. The Primal Way is quite different from this ethos. The philosophy of Great Harmony has it that everything belongs together as a whole and all parts are equally important for overall health. Hyemeyohsts Storm of the Cheyenne writes in *Seven Arrows:*

"One Half of you loves, and the Other Half of you at times hates. This is the Forked Medicine Pole of Man. The clever thing the Medicine has taught us here is this. One Half of you must understand the Other Half or you will tear yourself apart. It is the same with the Other Half of any People who live together. One must understand the Other, or they will destroy each other. But remember! Both Halves must try to understand. Even within yourself it is hard to know which of the Forks is which. 'Now why did I do that?' One Half of you asks the Other Half. You do things quite often which you do not mean to say or do, sometimes to yourself and sometimes to others. But you would not kill yourself for these mistakes, would you? I am quite certain that you would not. Yet there are those who have done this, who have killed either themselves or others. These are men who have not learned. An entire People can be like this. These People and men are not Full, they are not Whole . . .

"These People had been taught by the Black Robes [Christian missionaries] that good and evil existed as separate things. We talked with them about this philosophy and discovered their confusion. They had these two things set apart. But they are not separate. These things are found in the same Forked Tree. If One Half tries to split itself from the Other Half, the Tree will become crippled or die. These People we discovered were trying to split these things with law. Rather than taking this barren Way, we must tie together the paradoxes of our Twin Nature with the things of One Universe." [1]

The Forked Medicine Tree stands at the center of the Medicine Wheel and symbolizes the primal power of life. It is the World Tree, an archetypical motif for our rottenness in the Sacred Circle of Life. Splitting the Tree is breaking the Circle of Life. Western philosophy breaks the Circle and thus cripples human nature. The Black Robes teach the Christian mythos in which Eve, the primordial woman who is a motif of the Great Goddess living in Eden, is said to have eaten of the Tree. Christian theology splits the Tree with law, setting up a division of good at war with evil. This fragmentation of Nature with the artifact of law yields perversion of natural goodness. We are thus ejected out of the garden by are own invention.

In the *Republic*, Plato builds his moral position around the myth of Gyges. In this myth Gyges is a man who discovers a ring that gives him the power of invisibility. With this newly discovered power he immediately commits an Oedipus-like crime: he subdues the queen and with her help kills the king, and then takes the king place. Based on this myth Plato goes on to say that anyone with such power would do as he want, "no one could endure to hold from another's goods and not touch, when it was in his power to take what he would even out of the market without fear, and to go into any house and lie with anyone he wished, and to kill or set free from prison those he might wish, and to do anything else in the world like a very god . . . . Surely one would call this a strong proof that no one is just willingly but only under compulsion, believing that it is not a good to him personally; since whatever each thinks he will be able to do injustice, he does injustice." [2]

---

[1]   Storm, *Seven Arrows*. 124-125

[2]   Rouse, *Great Dialogues of Plato*, 156-157

The story of Gyges is like the story of Oedipus in that in both the king is killed and the killer has sex with the queen. In the case of Oedipus, the king is father and the queen is mother. Using this story as metaphor, Freud postulates his theory of the Oedipus complex, which asserts that young boys have sexual attraction to their mothers, and view their fathers as competition for their mothers' affection. Freud believed that the Oedipus complex is cross-culturally universal, and that it is continuous within the unconscious of the adult male necessitating that it be repressed so as to maintain an ethical social order.

There may very well be an Oedipus complex at the core of civil ethos, but it is not universal to all cultures. The Oedipus complex is a reaction formation resulting from psychic trauma originating from social imprinting shaped by patriarchal values. In other words, at a deeper level than the Oedipus complex is a subcurrent of psychic trauma related to the killing of the Great Mother Goddess. We may name this the *Orestes Project* from the Greek plays by Aeschylus in which Orestes kills his mother. When Orestes is on trial for having killed his mother, as part of his defense it is clamed that motherhood is not the true source of life, that life come from the father and therefore the mother is not the parent of her children. As evidence of this Athena is made to testify that she has no mother, but was born solely of Zeus. But this is a lie as we discover from the *Theogony* of Hesiod, which informs us that Metis, the goddess of wisdom, is the mother of Athena. Zeus swallowed Metis when she was pregnant with Athena, thus patriarchy consumes and assimilates the Goddess claiming her power as his.

Also in Hesiod's *Theogony* we find that the ancestor of all the gods is the Great Mother Earth, that she is the creator, and that she created out of herself Father Sky. In other words, Father Sky is the son of the Mother Earth, and they mate to produce the other deities. This is a very old and geographically wide spread motif belonging to the gynocentric religions—that the Mother produces out of herself a son who becomes her consort and lover. With the Orestes Project the old myths are re-mythed to serve as propaganda to delegitimatize the old ways for the sake of imposing a new political order. Thus we have Oedipus as the re-mything of an earlier motif with a reversal of values. With monotheism all this is forgotten and only god the Father is recognized.

Seven Arrows tells a story in which a mother and son share sexual love. With this story we find a very different ethno-psychology than that implied by Freud. The son subdues the mother who allows the interaction to become sexual. When later she shares this with her community, a woman in the camp objected saying that it was an "unreal thing" that this mother did. Another within the camp defends the mother saying that there are those who accept "war and its killing . . . lies, deceit, and greed . . . that these are the things that are unreal."[3] Incest is something not accepted in just about all cultures, and there is no difference here. However there is quite a difference in the attitude one may hold in relation to it.

Anthropologists have written on the universality of the so called "incest taboo." I think they are projecting their own cultural bias on others and not seeing what is truly there. Tribal cultures have clan systems that prescribe who may mate with whom, but the maintenance of this is not based on imposed enforcement, but from a respect for tradition and community. In any case it seems that Western psychology is rooted in the fear that apart from enforced taboos there would be a sexual free-fall with every kind of abomination and perversion. I submit for consideration that if there were no condemnation of incest or any laws or rules regarding such, there would be extremely little to no incest occurring as almost everyone would not be predisposed to such behaviors.

The study in *Seven Arrows* is a myth written by Storm to make a point about the morality taught by the white-man. On such he writes that "there is no such thing as good and bad. This is only a tool used by the white-men to create fear among themselves. It is only the man who searches for good who will also discover things he will perceive as bad. If this man then tries to dictate his own perception of what is good to others, he will ultimately become a bad man himself."[4]

In *Seven Arrows* what is being said is that, although one may at times do bad, overall we are good and can mostly be trusted as such, and that one does not need a moral education to be good, indeed such

---

3   Storm, *Seven Arrows,*152-153

4.   Stom, *Seven Arrows.* 126

an education will produce the opposite effect. In the myth of Gyges what is being said is that no one is good willingly, that goodness is something that must be imposed into our person against our natural impulses. This notion of being fundamentally bad is foundational to Plato's philosophy of education. He asserts that because one is born predisposed to being bad, it is the function of education to force one to become good by way of changing one's inborn nature.

In the *Laws* Plato states that, "the earliest sensations that a child feels in infancy are pleasure and pain." This he clams is the route by which virtue and vice first enters the soul. In Platonism vice is a product of living for bodily passions, and virtue is obtained when one moves beyond the bodily into the world of pure reason. Hence Plato asserts that if the child is left to follow his own pleasures she or he will live in vice, whereas to become virtuous she or he must be made so by reason. Therefore the original nature of the child must be altered. Education for Plato is aimed at the so-called, "correct formation of our feeling of pleasure and pain, which makes us hate what we ought to hate from the first to last, and love what we ought to love." [5]

What it is that we ought to hate is bodily pleasure, because the following of it leads to vice. That would be painful. Thus what Plato calls for under the name of education is that we ought to find pleasure in a certain kind of pain and pain in certain kinds of pleasure. That is to say, education calls for a reversal of the original state that we were born with.

In the political and educational philosophy of John Locke we have an echoing of Platonism stated in Judeo-Christian terms. Locke states that the child is born without the faculty of reason and must through education be made rational. Locke sees reason as god's Law, whereas what is without reason is godless or of the devil. As such, he suggests that the child is born bad and through reason must be made to be good. Hence the child is to have "no will of his own" until he is "subdued and improved" and brought up into the light of reason. Locke uses this same notion with his economic thinking, for nature itself is fallen from god law as a conquest of original sin, thus nature has become irrational and likewise must be subdued and improved by reason. Women in like manner are more like nature and thus not

---

5   Saunders, *Plato: The Law.* 85-86

as rational as man, therefore women ought not to have their own will but must be governed by men.

In Christianity we are told that when god created the world it was good, but when Eve ate of the fruit of the tree of knowledge of good and evil, sin entered into the world. Thus salvation consists in escaping from the natural world and entering into a heavenly state of pure reason. When all was unborn the world was good, but with Eve came birth and with birth came nature, and with nature came evil (the etymology of the word "nature" is from the Latin "natura" which means "to be born").

In Locke we read: "The law that was to govern Adam was the same that was to govern all his posterity—the law of reason. But his offspring having another way of entrance into the world, different from him, by a natural birth that produced them ignorant and without the use of reason, they were not presently under that law." [6]

This then is the "law" which the "Black Robes" used in splitting nature. This duality is an artifact of a schizoid mind fragmenting nature. It is both the origin and result of a neurotic repression of organic impulses. It is a denial of id out of fear and hate of it. The "law" is sublimation—the act of altering nature for the sake of anti-life politics. Plato writes:

"And ought not the rational principle, which is wise, have the care of the whole soul, to rule, and the passionate or spirited principle to be the subject and ally? . . . And him we call wise who has in him that little part which rules, and which proclaims there commands; that part too being supposed to have a knowledge of what is for the interest of each of the three parts and of the whole? And would you not say that he is temperate who has these same elements in friendly harmony, in whom the one ruling principle of reason, and two subject ones of spirit and desire are equally agreed that reason ought to rule, and do not rebel?" [7]

Dostoevsky writes in *Notes from Underground*: "You see gentlemen, reason is an excellent thing, there's no disputing that, but reason is nothing but reason and satisfies only the rational side of man's nature, while will is a manifestation of the whole life, that is,

---

[6] Locke, Two Treatise of Government. 148

[7] Wilbur and Allen, *The Worlds of Plato and Aristotle.* 52-57

of the whole human life including reason and all the impulses. And although our life, in this manifestation of it, is often worthless, yet it is life and not simply extracting square roots. Hence I, for instance, quite naturally want to live, in order to satisfy all my capacities for life, and not simply my capacity for reasoning, that is, not simply one twentieth of my capacity for life. What does reason know? Reason only knows what it has succeeded in learning (some things, perhaps, it will never learn; this is a poor comfort, but why not say so frankly?) and human nature acts as a whole, with everything that is in it, consciously or unconsciously, and, even if it goes wrong, it lives." [8]

The will, in the context that Dostoevsky seems to mean the term, is part and parcel of the passions and related to the id. This sense of the word seem a radial departure from Platonism. The will is here ontologically primal. It is akin to the Medicine of the Medicine Wheel. Out of it grows everything that consciousness is. The core of conscious existence and life is will. The worlding of worlds as we live it are acts of will. This does not mean that there are no realities outside of our willing as such, but what we allow to enter into ourselves and how we understand such are acts of will. When we oppose the will, and try to alter its nature, we neurotically frustrate ourselves. This results in perverted feelings and aggressive thoughts. In other words, the act of "rational" sublimation creates the very evil that it allegedly exists to correct.

What motivates much of philosophy is a sense that something is not right with regard to how one is living. Plato and Locke asserted that we somehow have fallen out of perfection. They saw society as existing in a wrong way, and so put forth agendas to set things right. They did not go deeply enough into the core of the problem; so instead of coming out with solutions they instead compounded the problem.

Like the philosophers of the West, those of the East perceived that something had run amuck. A major difference of assumption however occurs between the Far East and the West; whereas most Western philosophers assumed that the origin of the problem lay in the badness of human nature, most Far Easterners assumed that human nature is essentially good and that the bad in human behavior

---

[8]   Kaufmann, *Existentialism: From Dostoevsky to Sartre*, 65-66

is societal in origin. The Far Eastern perspective is that when human society is in harmony with Nature, then human behavior tends to be good; but when society falls out of harmony with Nature, a perversion of essential goodness follows and people behave badly.

Confucius, following this Far Eastern perspective, attempted to reform society so that it would be in accord with the Natural Way. He believed that the condition of society had so morally degenerated that it was perverting natural goodness. He maintained that if society were to recover it would be necessary to cultivate natural goodness in the people—especially the people in political power. This then is the task of Confucian education.

Lao-tzu also believed in natural goodness, but took exception to notions of social reform of the kind advocated by Confucius. Lao-tzu seemed to be saying that if the people are to recover their natural goodness and societies recover the Way, it will be necessary to remove the social influences that pervert nature. The solution is not in what one does, but in what one does not do. He implied that the proposed solution put forth by Confucius would not solve the problem but only make it worse.

The Way is what happens in and of itself without being made to do so. Nature apart from man-made culture effortlessly follows along the lines of least resistance. There are ecological niches and cosmic teleologies to all events. When everything follows the Way, then there is harmony. Philosophical Taoism maintains that man-made society has parted from the Way. This is in part because unnatural political institutions miseducate the people. That is to say, we are educated to follow artificiality rather than inborn nature. To recover the natural state we must become uneducated of the artificiality and become spontaneously nature-directed.

The fundamental difference between Confucianism and Philosophical Taoism is this: whereas the former asserts that there are social schemas to guide society into benevolence, the latter maintains that the only thing society can do to recover natural goodness is to do nothing that in any way would interfere with the growth of inborn nature. Hence Taoism states that by letting things be in their own innate way, solutions will come of themselves.

The educational philosophy of Rousseau has a lot in common with Taoism. Accordingly, education ought to be an effortless process of discovering one's natural capacities. Rousseau, in contradiction to Locke, asserts that, "the child's will ought not to be opposed." Like Lao-tzu, Rousseau believed that civilization has a corrupting influence on the mind of the child. Indeed civilization itself is sick and corrupt. In his theory of the "noble savage," Rousseau suggested that we were better off living in the state-of-nature. He wished to recover that benevolent state of nature as a suitable environment for the education of children. In contrast he felt that the classroom of the traditional school was definitely the wrong place for educating the child. Away from the city and into the woods, free and at large with nature is the preferred way. Working with the raw senses in an active way in a natural setting is the best place for early education.

The closest implementation of the Rousseauian ideal in a modern educational setting is Summerhill, founded in 1921 by A.S. Neill in England. Neill emphatically stated, "learning should come after play." He goes on to say, "children, like adults, learn what they want to learn." And so Summerhill is a free school where children are allowed to play or learn as they feel they want. Neill maintained that forced learning either does not work or if it does it does so at the cost of making children neurotic.

Those who oppose Rousseauian educational philosophy and the Summerhill School argue that there are some things that simply must be learned whether or not the child wants to learn, and that if one does not force the child to learn, then more often then not she or he will not; that if such results in some measure of psychological damage, then that is a necessary evil for the long-term good. In anticipation of such an argument Rousseau writes:

"Your first duty is to be human. Love childhood. Look with friendly eyes on its games, its pleasures, it amiable dispositions. Which of you does not sometime look back regretfully on the age when laughter was ever on the lips and the heart free of care? Why steal from the little innocents the enjoyment of a time that passes all too quickly?

"Already I hear the clamour of the false wisdom that regards the present as of no account and is forever chasing a future which flees as we advance. This is the time to correct the evil inclinations of mankind, you reply. Suffering should be increased in childhood when it is least felt, to reduce it at the age of reason. But how do you know that all the fine lessons with which you oppress the feeble mind of the child will not do more harm than good? Can you prove that these bad tendencies you profess to be correcting are not due to your own misguided effort rather than to nature?"[9]

Neill refers to the kind of psychological attitude that is the consequence of traditional education as "anti-life." Traditional education throughout the civilized world results in repression, which spawns neurosis, which leads to anti-life attitudes. For Freud repression is a necessary discontent, for without it the id would have free reign and we would behave as violent savages. In other words, Freud held to a view that early mankind was and children are immoral and if not made to be moral would behave immorally. This view is shared by Locke and Plato, and is the dominant position within the history of Western civilization. Rousseau and Neill take exception, and current evidence from anthropology and child psychology supports them. With the Freudian assumptions of human nature falsified, there exists no adequate justification for the perpetuation of repressive moral education. Wilhelm Reich, a friend of Neill's, was one of the first in the Freudian school to break with the orthodoxy and put forth the position that repression is a disease that must be cured, and that once cured humanity will behave well. Reich and Neill maintained that the ego/superego repression of the id does not create moral virtue, but rather anti-life attitudes—that it is out of a free id that goodness comes forth. Consistent with Philosophical Taoism, Neill and Reich felt that perversion of human goodness originates from the political, and that to correct this problem we must be educated not to be politically outer-directed, but must allow ourselves to be inwardly self-directed. According to Neill:

"We are anti-life and pro-death if we are pawns of politicians, merchants, or exploiters. We are pawns because we were trained to seek life negatively, humbly fitting ourselves into an authoritative society, and ready to die for the ideals of our masters . . . When I use the word anti-life, I do not mean death-seeking. I mean fearing life more than fearing death . . . . To be anti-life is to be pro-authority, pro-church religion, pro-repression, pro-oppression, or at least subservient to these . . . Pro-life equals fun, games, love, interesting work, hobbies, laughter, music, dance, consideration for others, and faith in [hu]man[ity]. Anti-life equals duty, obedience, profit, and

---

[9]   Boyd, *The Emile of Jean Jacques Rousseau*. 33

power. Throughout history anti-life has won, and will continue to win as long as youth is trained to fit into present-day adult conceptions" [10]

In a parallel description, Neill refers to the free and unfree child. The free child is raised in a pro-life fashion, whereas the unfree child is raised in an anti-life sickness. The free child is like Rousseau's child whose will is unopposed, whereas the unfree child is Locke's child who has no will of his own, but is sublimated into anti-life politics. The free child grows naturally, whereas the unfree child is manufactured by a machinated society. The difference in education and cultural upbringing makes the difference in attitude.

Most educational reforms are superficial in that they do not address the core of the problem. They simply assume the aims of society as given without regard to their moral implications and psychological impacts. Teachers all too often are technicians in the employment of politically programmed automatons whose task it is to produce a population of automatons. When the state authorities approach problems like juvenile delinquency or student discipline, they look for techniques to bring the youth in line with the political without asking if the political is worthwhile. Paul Goodman put forth the criticism that Western culture is so out of touch with human nature that it sets up conditions in which growing up is absurd. Attempts are made to socialize youth without regard to whether such socialization is worth having. In the words of Goodman:

"I shall therefore take the opposite tack and ask, 'Socialization to what? To what dominant society and available culture?' And if this question is asked, we must at once ask the other question, 'Is the harmonious organization to which the youth are inadequately socialized, perhaps against human nature, or not worthy of human nature, and therefore there is difficulty in growing up?' If this is so, the disaffection of youth is profound and it will not be finally remediable by better techniques of socializing. Instead, there will have to be changes in our society and its culture, so as to meet the appetites and capacities of human nature, in order to grow up." [11]

In the civilized world we have come to expect youth to be rebellious. We have come to believe that this behavior is natural,

---

[10] Neill, *Summerhill.* 343-344

[11] Goodman, *Growing Up Absurd,* 10

but it may be that there is misunderstanding as to the nature of this rebellion. Modern psychology suggests that young people are only going through a phase, trying to find their identity or something like that. It should be noted that aboriginal societies outside of Western influence do not have youth rebellions as a general pattern. In fact aboriginal youth are happy to join with the adult world as a natural pattern of coming of age. Only in civilized societies and those approaching civil norms do we have youth rebellions. It seems to me that youth rebellions are natural responses against the artificiality of civil norms. We by nature want to be free! But the civil ethos demands conformity. Civil normality is the tyranny of an artificially constructed average, which is anti-natural. At adolescence the child enters the age where she or he naturally begins to assert her or his freedom, which is at odds with educational demands for conformity. More often than not in these days, civil demands win out over natural inclinations. With each win of civil ethos, humanity is diminished.

Goodman differentiates between sub-society and sub-culture. A sub-society is a natural subset of culture in which people group together out of common interests. A youth sub-society is one in which children get together to play, have fun, learn, and socialize, without being in opposition to the overall culture. A sub-culture is produced when a sub-society holds to values at odds with the dominant culture, and the dominant culture attempts to superimpose its values on the other. This is an unnatural state of affairs. When the youth and the elders of a society are at odds with one another, the culture is fragmented and the integrity of the community is undermined. The reason aboriginal societies do not have the problem of juvenile delinquency is that their cultures are whole and the youth and elders are integrated into one unified community.

For thousands of years before the advent of civilization our ancestors lived in tribal cultures. Everyone was sisters and brothers, daughters and sons, aunts and uncles, tribal family members all. There was an abundance of emotional support in the spirit of authentic sharing and caring. Everybody in the tribe took care of the educational needs of everyone else as part of the ordinary affairs of life. There was no school as a place set aside to send children; rather education took place any time a learning opportunity presented itself within the community as a whole. In this way children were meaningful members of the day-to-day life of the community. Learning was part of the doings of the people.

At the core of Native American education is the Medicine Wheel. To be whole in all one does is central to the Medicine Way. In whatever one does, be it social, personal, economical, or religious—the whole of one's being comes to center. To be centered means to draw all the parts of the Wheel into a harmony. Thinking, feeling, sensation and intuition all come to center. The organism and the ecology are unified. The individual and the societal are in friendly, loving inter-accommodation. Freedom is an essential part of being whole and healthy. Education in the aboriginal way is not a repressive imposition from one generation onto the next. Each generation is given freedom to make its own expression of itself. Tradition is carried on out of the youth's love-based respect for the elders—something that spontaneously happens when generations are bonded together in the spirit of sharing and caring. And if someone in the tribal family turns out not to fit well into the culture, more often then not the people will accommodate the difference rather then forcing the individual to conform. In describing Indian ways in contradiction to those of the West, Wilfred Pelletier of the Ottawa Indians said the following:

"One of the most important factors in human development is called curiosity; curiosity is, of course, one of the prime factors in the motivation of human beings. In talking about this I will mention one or two examples of differences between Indians and Whites. Most children are allowed to grow in an Indian community . . . When I said that children are allowed to grow in an Indian community, I mean they are allowed to pretty well do as they wish—to explore, discover for themselves on their own terms their own feelings and their own way, by observing and making decisions for themselves. In Western society, children are generally directed, taught how to behave, that is in certain places, certain time, with certain people, to certain people, etc. They are generally told what is good for them and so on, thereby removing curiosity from them. Now what this is really all about is that if curiosity as a means to motivation is removed, and unless it is replaced with something else—there won't be any action, so what white society attempts to do is replace this natural motivation of curiosity with incentives, that is, competitive incentives, and this goes all the way from good marks on your report card to the possession of a Cadillac car when you get a little older. But it's all the same system and designed to appeal to deficiency motivation and to protract and perpetuate deficiency motivation and which is essentially an immature condition so that people or most people in Western culture at the present time never know anything except deficiency motivation and spend their whole lives in trying to fill needs. The point here is that anyone whose entire attention is taken up with the filling of his personal needs, whether these are real or imaginary, is in no condition to give anything. I will not go into the subject of education here, except to say that the system as it now exists is a killing process. By this I mean killing psychologically and sometimes mentally. It has produced the environment of which we now find ourselves part. It has produced the statistics you talk about, the organizations both social and political, the isolation of every individual from another. I could go on and on talking about what the system has done and especially to children when they first enter these institutions we call schools. Not only is curiosity removed, but authoritarian figures dominate the place, and we call them teachers. They do not allow you to feel about something; they tell you how to feel about it. Can you imagine then—You're raised in a community, allowed to feel your way through life to the point when you become six or seven, then someone tells you all these things are not so, but this is how it is and that you are to be aggressive and you must compete—so does anyone help you understand these things, oh no—because you might then know what they know, and you too might get a star and so on" [12]

The curiosity that Pelletier speaks of is the natural playfulness of healthy humanity. It is what Neil refers to as pro-life freedom, with which one has "fun, games, love, interesting work, hobbies, laughter, music, dance, consideration for others," and the like. But civil ethos removes this pro-life curiosity and replaces it with anti-life moralism, asserting "duty, obedience, profit, and power" and the like. This pathology creates a void in the fiber of one's being. One comes to feel incomplete and compelled to continuously seeking fulfillment. This is what Maslow referred to a "d-cognition," the "d" standing for deficiency in much the same way the Pelletier uses the term, which is to say, that the person is so lacking in herself or himself that the

---

[12] Pelletier, *Two Articles*

whole psychic life is seeking but not finding satisfaction. It is like a person who is very thirsty drinking salt water—the more one drinks, the thirstier one gets and on and on with no satisfaction. This is the condition of the modern world driven by a deficiency psychology, forever wanting but never being satisfied. The deficiency that comes from anti-life indoctrination yields this disease in which one seeks to fill the void of inner feeling with the trappings of external consumerism. The more one seeks to fill desires in outer things, the more deficiency one experiences in the essential joy of being. The joy of being is what Maslow called "b-cognition" the "b" standing for "being," as in the state of psychological health in and through self-actualization. The Way of "being" is the antidote to d-cognition. The Way of recovery is unlearning, becoming free from deficiency-generated desires and being with the fullness of the joy of life, spontaneously natural.

In Philosophical Taoism there is the notion of being without desire. What is meant here is artificially generated desire. Organic pleasure as given by Nature is one with the Way. The desirelessness of Taoism is not, as with Platonism, a denial of the id, rather it is being so fully with the id that one is full and therefore without deficiency. This fullness takes one beyond dependence on consumer materialism. One is fully with the body, living with the freedom of the Way with openness to the totality of being. Following in the tradition of Lao-tzu, the Taoist philosopher *Chuang-tzu* is attributed as saying:

"In the case of the body, it is best to let it go along with things. In the case of the emotions, it is best to let them follow where they will. By going along with things, you avoid becoming separated from them. By letting the emotions follow as they will, you avoid fatigue. And when there is no separation or fatigue, then you need not seek any outward adornment or depend upon the body [as object]. And when you no longer seek outward adornment or depend upon the body, you have in fact ceased to depend upon any material thing." [13]

In Philosophical Taoism it is seen that there is a connection between artificial desire and socially induced knowledge. One seeks knowledge as a means to attain gratification related to desire. Knowledge of this kind is symptomatic of psychological deficiency. The kind of knowledge that emerges out of deficiency is thought

---

[13] Watson, *The Complete Works of Chuang tzu.* 216

dependent. Thinking divides phenomena into parts setting up a psychic duality in which separation is induced into the field of awareness. In the Natural Way there are no parts and no separation—all is one. Knowing the Way (which is knowledge of no knowledge) is not a product of thought. This is not to say that thinking in and of itself is at odds with the Way—thinking is a natural attribute of being human, but thinking out of balance with the other modes of consciousness is disharmonious. The problem comes about when thinking is given a priority over other modes of being. On the Medicine Wheel the priority of thought yields retardation of feeling. It is as Pelletier said, "essentially an immature condition." Knowing the Way is living in harmony. To my Cherokee ancestors before we were "Civilized," thinking—based knowledge was seen as disease. This is reflected in the following quote:

"In the tribal way, 'knowing' was to be in harmony and at peace with oneself and nature, while 'thinking' implied disharmony and evil. To their tribesmen, as these Cherokee writers illustrate, the 'thinker' was someone who harbored 'malign emotions,' for he created 'human disharmony with Nature.' It was this cosmic concept of ecology that tribal man always 'know,' modern man is still 'thinking about'" [14]

Lao-tzu taught that the way of the scholar is to learn something new daily, but the Way of the sage is to unlearn. Knowledge of the scholar comes from the outer world of things and social institutions. Knowing wisdom comes from deep within one's organic being. This is the meaning in Lao-tzu's teaching that without going outside or looking through windows one may know the whole world. It is on this point that Lao-tzu and Confucius differ. Confucius asserted the way of the scholar. For him learning was all important for the foundation of social order and morality. Lao-tzu asserted that knowledge fragments original nature, which produces deprivation of the tranquility of the Way. This in turn distorts virtue. When virtue is distorted, immorality follows. From *Lao-Tzu:*

> "When the great Way was abandoned,
>   Humanity and righteousness appeared.
>   When the intelligent and knowledgeable arose,

---

[14] Witt and Steiner, *The Way.* 119

Great hypocrisy appeared.
When the six relationships were not in harmony,
Filial piety and paternalistic kindness appeared.
When the state was in chaos and disorder,
Loyal ministers appeared.

Transcend sagacity and abandon intellect;
The people will be benefited a hundredfold.
Transcend humanity and abandon righteousness;
The people will return to filial piety and paternal kindness.
Transcend craftiness and abandon profit;
Robbers and thieves no longer will exist . . .

One with supreme virtue is not attached to virtue, so has virtue.
One with lower virtue does not lose virtue, so has no virtue.
One with supreme virtue is in non-action and acts without purpose.
One with lower virtue is in action and has purpose in his actions.
One with high humanity is in action but acts without purpose.
One with high righteousness is in action and acts with purpose.
One with high propriety is in action but, if people do not respond,
He raises armies to draw others to him.
Therefore, when people lose the Way, they resort to virtue.
Losing virtue, they resort to humanity.
Losing humanity, they resort to righteousness.
Losing righteousness, they resort to propriety.
Propriety marks the lack of loyalty and trust and the beginning of disorder!
The man with foreknowledge is only an ornament of the Way,
And the beginning of stupidity.
Therefore, the great man dwells on the thick, but not on the thin.
Dwells on the substance, but not on the ornament.
So, he renounces that and takes this." [15]

---

[15]   Wu, *The Book of Lao-tzu,* Chapters 18, 19, and 38

It has been said that there is no one more dangerous in the world than someone who wants to do good. Inquisitions, persecutions, executions, genocides, terrorism, crusades, endless wars for all kinds for righteous causes, and the list goes on and on of such activity committed by individuals who believed that they were doing "good." So Lao-tzu points out that those who are attached to virtue lose it. One becomes attached to virtue through making it an object of knowledge and desire. When virtue is fragmented by the thought dynamic of knowledge it is no longer authentic virtue. Confucian ethics is based on knowledge and calls for action and purpose. Lao-tzu taught that action and purpose based in knowledge yields disharmony with the Way. Action based on having no purpose and nonaction yields high humanity.

Humanity is the key value in Confucian ethics and apparently is important to Lao-tzu as well. For Lao-tzu one behaves humanely by not being conscious of trying to be humane. This is clearly a position antithetical to Confucius. For Confucius humanity requires knowledge of righteousness, and that is the standard for judging right and wrong. Propriety is thus what righteousness leads to—that is to say, with standards of right and wrong one may assert what constitutes proper behavior. A social order so constituted must somehow enforce its standards. So Lao-tzu points out that this civil ethos leads to violence. Part of the context in which Lao-tzu was teaching was a society becoming more and more violent. He was aware that earlier time had been more peaceful, and that the earliest time was most peaceful. He thus was seeing degeneration: from the loss of virtue, people resort to humanity, losing humanity then righteousness, then propriety, followed by disorder, greed, violence, and so forth.

The Confucionists also believed that earlier time had been better, and so advocated a return to those ways. They believed this might happen through moral education. The Taoist believed that the Confucian educational philosophy is not a solution, but part of the problem. On the negative impact of moral education Neill is in agreement with Taoism, which is to say, the Natural Way works best without intuitional interference. Writes Neill:

"The newborn child brings with him a life force; his will, his unconscious urge is to live. His life force prompts him to eat, to explore his body, to gratify his wishes. He acts as Nature intended him to act, as he was made to act. But, to the adult, the will of God in the child—the will of Nature in the child—is the will of the devil. Practically every adult believes that the nature of the child must be improved. Hence it happens that every parent begins to teach the young child how to live. The child soon comes up against a whole system of prohibitions. This is naughty and that is dirty and such and such is selfish. The original voice of the child's natural life force meets the voice of instruction. The church would call the voice of Nature the voice of the devil, and the voice of moral instruction the voice of God. I am convinced that the names should be reversed. I believe that it is moral instruction that makes the child bad. I find that when I smash the moral instruction a bad boy has received, he becomes a good boy." [16]

The newborn child is born with the Way and its virtue. The Way is within the life-force and virtue of the child's will. When sociopolitical conditions interfere with inborn nature then virtue is lost. The voice of instruction leads to hypocrisy. The original voice of the child's natural life-force does not need instruction in order to be good. To be with the Way is to be as the uncarved block, which is to be as a newborn child. In the biblical narrative evil enters into the world by way of free will, thus freedom is not trusted. The devil is the personification of the paranoia of politically indoctrinated anti-life mankind. More generally in the history of civilization the devil is the god of the enemy. This moral dualism is a product of societies that are defined by a history of warfare—culture in which education is akin to military training. The historical root of god in Jewish history was that of a war totem. Early Hebrew history is a story of how they invaded the lands of others committing genocide against them and demonizing their deities. To the extent that this is the root of monotheism, and the religious foundation of Christian morality, something destructive of life became idealized as good, and something positive about living become personified as evil. Neill by reversing this is restoring the original religion of God as Goddess—affirming the goodness of life.

---

[16]   Neill, *Summerhill*, 250

THE WAY OF THE NORTH: WISDOM
OF THE ELDERS

Early in the twentieth century a group of German ethnographers traveled through Samoa, collecting data. One of their hosts was a chief named Tuiavii of the village Tiavea on the island of Upolu. When the ethnographers went back to Germany, Tuiavii went with them. Upon his return to Samoa, he gave talks to his people about his experience in Europe. He described the Europeans as "people with weird tastes. For no reason at all, they do all kinds of things that make them sick." The Samoans refer to people who come from the outside world as "Papalagi," which means, "sky buster." In their worldview the world is seen as existing under a great sky dome. It would be trivializing to say this is not scientific. Phenomenologically the sky does seem like a dome. It is true enough as appearance goes, and that is good enough to speak about what needs to be spoken. In a manner of speaking people coming in from beyond must pass through the dome. Moreover what the Europeans brought with them was so different from indigenous ways that they did burst through from a very different world.

What Tuiavii saw of European society convinced him that the old ways of his people were better. Much of what he said is consistent with what other indigenous people have said in reference to civilization. Also there is consistency between indigenous voices and Philosophical Taoism. What Tuiavii had to say is congruent with what Lao-tzu in all likelihood would have said given a similar context. One difference is that Lao-tzu was a civilized scholar who came to reject civilization in preference for the Primal Way. Tuiavii lived the Primal Way from the start, and then came to view civilization as an outsider.

Having entered an urban environment in Europe, this indigenous sage describes it as follows:

"These stone crates with all those people, these deep fissures of stone intertwining like long rivers, the hustle and bustle, the black smoke and the dirt floating overhead without one single tree, without a spot of blue sky or nice clouds, all this together is called "town" by the Papalagi . . .

"In these streets enormous glass boxes are built, in which all sorts of things are laid out that the Papalagi needs for his living: loincloths, hand and footskins, head-ornaments, foodstuffs, meat and also real fruits and vegetables and many other things. Those things are laid out in a way so that everyone can see them and they appear very inviting. But nobody is allowed to take anything from there, even if he needs it very badly, only after getting permission first and after making a sacrifice . . .

"In our language 'lau' means 'mine,' but it also means 'your.' It's almost the same thing. But in the language of the Papalagi, it is hard to find words that differ so much in meaning as 'mine' and 'your.' . . .

"The Papalagi are in need of laws guarding their mine, because otherwise, the people with little or no mine at all would take it away from them. Because if there are people that claim a lot for themselves, there are always a lot of others left standing empty handed . . .

"Brothers! What is your opinion of a man who has a big house, big enough to lodge an entire Samoan village, and who doesn't permit a traveler to spend the night under his roof? What do you think of a man who holds an entire bunch of bananas in his hands and who is unwilling to give even a single fruit to the starving man who pleads for it? I can see the anger flaring up in your eyes and the contempt coming to your lips. Know then that the Papalagi act this way every hour, every day. Even if he has a hundred mats, he won't give away a single one to his brother who has none. No, he even blames his brother for having none. Even if his hut is stuffed to the roof with food, so much that he and his aiga [family] cannot eat it in years, he will not even go look for his brothers who have nothing to eat and looks pale and hungry. And there are many pale and hungry Papalagi." [17]

---

[17] Scheurmann, *The Papalagi.* 5-16

Consumer materialism is an invention of civilization. The notion of property is inconsistent with primal ethos. Indigenous people belong to the land, but the land belongs to no one. Everything one has in this life is a gift from the Great Sprit, and as a gift must be shared. In a Samoan village or a traditional American Indian community everything is shared, whereas if anything is not in use it is free to be used by others. Part of the social psychology of this is that one's sense of personal identity is not individualistic, as it is in the West, but is socially oriented. Of primal people it may be said that self and tribe are one, whereas what is good for the tribe is good for self. Accordingly, ownership is collective and for the good of all the people. Part of what constitutes the good of the People is that each person is provided for, without interference with freedom. Freedom does not mean the right to accumulate personal wealth. No one has the right to own so much that by so doing such interferes with the ability of others to have a decent living. Activity of excessive accumulation of wealth by a few individuals divides societies and destroys social togetherness. It also destroys freedom in that one becomes a slave to economics, which robs humanity of the joy of living.

In the language of the Sioux the word that is comparable to "Papalagi" is "Wasichu." This word means something like "he who lives off the fat of the land." The American Indians noticed that the Wasichus would steal all they could from the land, exploiting it for all it was worth and giving nothing back. Wasichu thus means greedy ones. When Black Elk of the Sioux was in Europe late in the ninetieth century, he observed the following:

"I could see that the Wasichus did not care for each other the way our people did before the nation's hoop was broken. They would take everything from each other if they could, and so there were some who had more of everything than they could use, while crowds of people had nothing at all and maybe were starving. They had forgotten that the earth was their mother. This could not be better than the old way of my people" [18]

Lao-tzu agrees with Tuavii and Black Elk on the ill effects of having some who own much while others have little or nothing. Lao-tzu

---

[18] Neihardt, *Black Elk Speaks.* 221

appears to think that economic activity of excess yields conditions of poverty—also that such activity is contrary to the Way.

"The people are starving
Because those above tax them too heavily.
Therefore, they starve.
The people are hard to govern
Because those above are too active.
Therefore, they are hard to govern.
The people make light of death
Because those above seek too much for their own lives.
Therefore, they make light of death . . .

Is not the way of Heaven like the stringing of a bow?
The upper part is depressed,
The lower part is raised;
The too-long string is shortened,
The too-short string is added to.
The way of Heaven reduces excesses and make up deficiencies.
The path of man is not so;
It decreases the deficient to supply the excessive." [1]

Elders in traditional American Indian communities have told me that one may identify the chiefs as the ones who are poorest. This because as leaders they look out for the needs of others and give much away to help the people. In many tribes there is a rite of the Give-Away. This rite happens at social gathering where the people come together for dancing and singing, and then those who have much give gifts to others who have less. The underlying philosophy is that it is not good to have much when others have little. It has been my personal experience in Indian communities in which I have lived and visited that everyone is taken care of to the limits of what is possible and nobody goes without so long as there is something to share; and this is in communities that are among the poorest in North America. Of course much of the poverty is a direct consequence of the genocidal activity of government that takes by force or deception

---

[1]   Wu, *The Book of Lao-tzu*, chapter 75 and 77

to enrich those who already have too much. In the old days there was no poverty among the Indians.

It is the propaganda of capitalism that before modern times everyone lived in poverty, but that now a few have gained wealth, and they in turn create additional opportunities for others to do the same. The reality is much different. Before the European invasion of America the Indians lived a life of abundance in which no one was without what was needed to live a good life. It is capitalist greed that robbed others of their labor and resources so they could have excessive wealth and power. Poverty is a product of capitalism, along with exploitation of people and resources and degeneration and destruction of ecology.

Samoa was one of the last places on earth to be impacted by the colonial global economy. When I was living there in the 1980s much of the old ways were still in place. When I visited a village I was brought into the homes and treated with great generosity. The wealth of kindness was abundant in ways I have seldom seen in Westernized communities. There was no hunger or homelessness in this one of the poorest countries in the world. I call them poor, but this is misleading, for they were a people who did not experience much in the way of want. They just did not have much of a money-based economy, and not much need for one given their self-reliance on traditional ways. Their wealth was in sharing and caring, and the joy of community life. Upon my return to the United States I had the experience of standing on a street corner seeing the limousine of the U.S. vice president go by followed by a party of luxury cars with police escort, and on that same street there were many homeless people sleeping on the street or begging for money.

In the Western world it is said that time is money. Time in the modern West is a threefold fragmentation of past, present and future. Time is thought of as linear movement along a line from left to right. It is part of the up-and-to-the-right orientation, which breaks out of the Circle of Life. Primal time is cyclical, whereas everything returns to its point of origin. In Taoism this is the principle of reversion: "Reversal is the movement of the Way." When time is cyclical, all is eternal now. There is nowhere to go, because all paths lead back from the place they begin. Nature as such is sacred and cannot be improved. But when time is a linear progression forever leaving the past and heading to a future of unlimited possibilities, then it may be said that things may be forever improved—an endless path of desires with no fulfillment.

The modern world began with a restructuring of space and time. In space an analytic grid of perspective geometry is superimposed on the visual field. This is the technique employed by Renaissance artists in creating a new fashion of art, a photo-realism that displaced the more theo-centric symbolic art of the medieval. Renaissance art gave birth to the modern world by redefining the way the world was understood. With this modern way of seeing, the visual field was fragmented into little bites that could be conceptually taken apart and reassembled at the will of some master planner. This is the precursor to the development of analytical geometry which is foundational to the development of calculus, which is the language of modern physics, which in turn is the dominant epistemology of technology. With this the world becomes dissected, killing the life of the whole. Time is likewise fragmented into bites: seconds, minutes, hours, and so forth. At the beginning of the modern world mechanical clocks were installed in bell towers all over Europe. With this everybody in town was made constantly aware of the time. Work schedules were made progressively more efficient with every improvement in time measuring technology. Clocks appeared everywhere and with that everyone become a slave to them. The clock even became a metaphor for the nature of the universe—the clock like nature of modern physics. With this we had the making of industrial society, and with that came exploitation and alienation. This modality of time drives the joy of life out of humanity and turns people into automations. In *For Every North American Indian,* a collection of essays written by Indians we read the following:

"I don't much like looking back at what happened to me at school. It seems to me that the only things I enjoyed was playing hooky and running away. One of the difficult things I had to cope with was something called time. The teacher would talk about wasting time. I didn't know how you could waste time. And then she would say you could make it up, you could make up time. She'd read us a story in school and then she'd say we've lost all that time, so now we have to hurry and make it up. I couldn't figure out what that meant, either. There were all kinds of things about time that bewildered me. I did not understand what all this clock watching was about, because in our community we ate when we were hungry and slept when we felt tired. We did not do things on any kind of schedule, yet that never presented a problem. The things that were necessary always got done.

"I discovered gradually that the White people lived in two kinds of time, the past and the future. Indians, on the other hand, lived in an eternal present. Our history only ran back to the oldest member of the community, so there was no way we could live in the past or the future, we could only live in the here and now. When we become like you people [white-man], dealing with the past, trying to live some kind of future that doesn't exist, then we'll have taken ourselves completely out of the present." [2]

Tuiavii believed that the white-man's temporal orientation was a kind of disease, because it keeps him dissatisfied. Modern people can never just be in the here and now, but must always be planning, always thinking about what to do next, or living in memories. In Indian country there is what we call "Indian-time," which means that we get around to doing whatever it is that we need to do whenever we get around to doing it, but things got done that needed to get done, and people enjoyed one another's company in the process. The white-man calls this being lazy, but I have been told that it is the white society that is lazy in always forcing itself to do that which is not wanted, keeping active in such a way as to promote the unhappiness of everyone. Such continuous and excessive activity becomes a means of being in denial of the existential crisis that such a life-style creates. I guess misery likes company, because when the white-men saw others living in a different way, they imposed on these others the Euro-centric notion of normality. And so it is becoming a global phenomenon whereas everywhere one travels these days it is more and more culturally homogenous in conformity to the invention of Western society.

The technology of time measurement yields machination of society and consciousness. Modern humanity is programmed by the clock. In the industrial world machinery is everywhere and controls every aspect of modern life. The factory system provides

---

[2]   Pelletier, *For Every North American Indian*. 27

us with most of what we own. We have become producers and consumers—component parts of a machinated society. In a mass society we have been reduced to numbers and so much data. Today government is about mechanical manipulation of population. The person is lost in the mass. Less and less is personal and more and more is machine produced. Tuiavii understood the dehumanizing effects of machines:

"A machine may make all sorts of things with its strong hand, but during its labor it eats out all the love that is present in the things we make with our hands. What do I care for a canoe that is cut out for me by a machine, a cold lifeless machine that is unable to talk about its product, that doesn't smile when the product is finished and can not take its product to his father or mother to have it admired. Would I be able to love my tanoa [wooden bowl] like I love her now, when a machine could make me another any moment, without my intervention? That's the big curse of the machine; the Papalagi love nothing anymore, because the machine can make them a new one anytime. They have to feed it their own life blood in order to receive its heartless miracles." [3]

Taoist teachings are congruent with Tuavii's views of the effects of machination. In *Chuang-tzu* we read: "where there are machines, there are bound to be machine worries; where there are machine worries, there are bound to be machine hearts. With a machine heart in your breast, you've spoiled what was pure and simple; and without the pure and simple, the life of the spirit knows no rest. Where the life of the spirit knows no rest, the Way will cease to buoy you up." [4]

There is a social psychology to epistemology. The very act of learning mechanics, be it engineering, computers, driving a car, viewing television, or the like, structures consciousness in a way that tends to make it mechanical. This machination of consciousness yields machine inspired worries and makes thinking go against organic wisdom. Such a heart/mind becomes like a machine—this is the essence of intellectualism in the modern world. The driving force of modern life is intellect. Modern history is the history of intellectual ideas shaping and reshaping society. Newtonian physics gave us

---

[3]   Scheurmann, *The Papalagi*. 27

[4]   Watson, The Complete Works of Chuang Tzu. 134

the paradigm of industrialization, and Einstein's ideas lead to the development of the atomic bomb. Like Philosophical Taoism and the philosophy of the primal Cherokees, Tuiavii views intellectualism as a kind of disease:

"The Papalagi think so much that for them thinking has become a habit, a necessity, and need. He has to keep on thinking. Only after much trouble does he succeed in not thinking and instead lives with his whole body at once . . . . Thinking thoughts (the fruit of thinking) keeps him enslaved, intoxicated by his own thoughts. When the sun is shining, all the time he thinks about how nicely it shines. That's wrong, foolishness! Because when the sun shines it is better not to think at all. A wise man would stretch out his limbs in the warm light and not give a thought in the meantime. He doesn't only absorb the sun with his head, but also with his hands and feet, his belly, his ankles and all his limbs. He lets his skin and his limbs do the thinking for him. For those parts think too, though not the way the head thinks . . . The only way to help those thought-patients is throwing away their thoughts, is forgetting. But they don't teach that and so hardly anybody can do it. Most of them carry so many thoughts inside their heads that it tires their bodies and makes them weak and wilted before their time." [5]

Lao-tzu taught to avoid identification with too much knowledge. Attachment to knowledge can and often does disrupt harmony with the Way. Knowledge is often a kind of sickness, and to become healthy may require un-learning.

> "To pursue learning is to increase daily.
> To practice the Way is to decrease daily . . .
>
> In ancient times, one who was good at practicing the Way
> Did not make the people clever
> But kept them in ignorance.
> If the people are hard to govern,
> It is because they have too much knowledge.
> Therefore, one who governs the state with knowledge
> Is a malefactor to the state.

---

[5] Scheurmann, *The Papalagi*. 38-39

One who does not govern the state with knowledge
Is a benefactor to the state . . .

One who knows, but does not know, is best.
One who does not know, but knows, is sick.
Only one who recognizes this sickness as sickness
Will not have sickness." [6]

The "heavy thinking sickness" as Tuiavii called it, is born out of anti-life values. Civil ethos overall and most especially in modernity is anti-organic. Hyper-intellectualism draws the life energy away from most of the body to concentrate it into the head. As with Plato's divided line, it separates the lower (body) from the upper (mind); then with the up-and-to-the-right of the ascending line, the body is denied and the mind is given all. The body is assumed as being the locus of evil. It threatens the status quo of pure rational thought. Sexual delight then becomes very threading to civil ethos. According to psychoanalytic theory, civilization is formed out of the sublimation of libido. Sexual energy is regulated and redirected towards the kind of work that is unnatural to life. It is as Plato put it, "finding pain in pleasure and pleasure in pain"—which is a reversal of our inborn natural condition. To go against that which we are by birth is to go against Nature.

Tuiavii noticed the extent to which Europeans are sexually oppressed, and also the extent to which they are sexually obsessed. He speculated that this was so because they deprive themselves of the enjoyment of physical pleasure and the beauty of the body. He suggested that if they allowed themselves the enjoyment of physical pleasures they "could focus their attention on other things." The relation between oppression and obsession is that the more oppressed one becomes the more obsessed one is of the object of repression. Moreover the oppression/repression of sexual energy causes pathological behavior to manifest. Normally one does not find pornography, prostitution or molestation of children in aboriginal societies. All these are mostly found in sexually oppressed cultures. Also promiscuity is more common among the sexually oppressed

---

[6]   Wu, *The Book of Lao-tzu*, Chapters 48, 65, 71

as a reaction to the denial of appropriate means of gratification. All cultures have boundaries of appropriate behavior, but in oppressed populations the sexual energy takes on an unconscious dynamic and appropriateness lost.

With civil ethos we have a hate/fear of sex. At the same time, given the depravity that this hate/fear creates, there is an obsession for sex. Much of modern culture turns sex into an object of commercial consumption. Women are sexually exploited, as the earth is raped. Sex is a big industry in an economic system based on the denial of sexual freedom. The nude body is regarded as obscene, and so also are sexual acts. The word 'fuck' and other such words cannot be spoken on the pubic airwaves and in certain kinds of social occasions. There is a great deal of superstition in the West about sex; for example, the enjoyment of sex may lead to a breakdown of morality. It is closer to the truth to say that the absence of sexual gratification leads to loss of moral goodness.

A study by neuropsychologist James Prescott showed that sexually repressed cultures tend to be more violent, whereas sexually free cultures tend to be happier, healthier, and more peaceful. The manner in which children are raised in relationship to physical pleasure or lack thereof has major significance to overall emotional well-being and the ability as an adult to enjoy sexuality. He writes, "The reciprocal relationship of pleasure and violence is highly significant because certain sensory experiences during the formative periods of development will create a neuropsychological predisposition for either violence-seeking or pleasure-seeking behaviors later in life. I am convinced that various abnormal social and emotional behaviors resulting from what psychologists call 'maternal-social' deprivation, that is, a lack of tender loving care, are caused by a unique type of sensory deprivation, *somatosensory* deprivation." [7]

Margaret Mead's study of Samoa brought her to the belief that traditional Samoan culture is healthier than Euro-American society. Her Samoan study focused on the question of adolescent development. It was assumed by developmental psychologists of the time that adolescence is by nature a period of psycho-emotional turbulence

---

[7]   Prescott, "Body Pleasure and the Origins of Violence," *Bulletin of the Atomic Scientist,* Nov 1975.

and identity crisis. In Western society this is the case, but Mead's findings show that this is not the case in traditional Samoa—for them the transition from childhood to adulthood is smooth and a time of happiness. If adolescence were a time of turbulence and crisis by nature, then it would follow that it would be so for all societies without exception; however if there is but one exception, then it follows that it is not so by nature, thus a problem involving social circumstances. Mead provides one exception. Since then the number of exceptions has multiplied as social scientists discover the absence of adolescent crisis in many cultures around the world. Adolescent crisis appears to be a phenomenon of civil ethos. For primal societies no such crisis exists.

Mead also noticed the absence of neurosis in Samoa. Again, neurosis appears to be mostly a phenomenon of civil ethos. For aboriginal societies neurosis does not have a significant presence. According to psychoanalytic theory, neurosis results when libido is repressed into unconsciousness. Insofar as sexual energy is the energy of life, neurosis is anti-life. For Freud, neurosis was a necessary condition for social order. Wilhelm Reich argued against Freud on this point, asserting that neurosis is a sickness that can be cured and that society can be healthy and neurosis free. As evidence of this Reich cites the observations of anthropologist Bronislaw Malinowski who studied the Trobriand Islanders. These islanders, like the Samoans, are sexually free and unrepressed, and are a neurosis free and healthy people. Writes Malinowski:

"The child's freedom and independence exist also to sexual matters. To begin with, children hear of and witness much in the sexual life of their elders. Within the house, where the parents have no possibility of finding privacy, a child has opportunities of acquiring practical information concerning the sexual act. I was told that no special precautions are taken to prevent children from witnessing their parents' sexual enjoyment . . .

"There are plenty of opportunities for both boys and girls to receive instruction in erotic matter from their companions. The children initiate each other into the mysteries of sexual life in a directly practical manner at a very early age. A premature amorous existence begins among them long before they are able really to carry out the act of sex. They indulge in play and pastimes in which they satisfy their curiosity concerning the appearance and function of the organs of generation, and incidentally receive, it would seem, a certain amount of positive pleasure. Genital manipulation and such minor perversions as oral stimulation of the organs are typical forms of this amusement. Small boys and girls are said to be frequently initiated by their somewhat older companions, who allow them to witness their own amorous dalliance. As they are untrammeled by the authority of their elders and unrestrained by any moral code, except that of specific tribal [incest] taboo, there is nothing but their degree of curiosity, of ripeness, and of temperament or sensuality, to determine how much or how little they shall indulge in sexual pastimes.

"The attitude of the grown-ups and even of the parents toward such infantile indulgence is either that of complete indifference or complacency—they find it natural, and do not see why they should scold or interfere. Usually they show a kind of tolerant and amused interest, and discuss the love affairs of their children with easy jocularity." [8]

One may think from the above quote that these islanders are sexually promiscuous. This however would be a misleading conclusion. There is a presupposition on the part of those who embrace anti-sex morality that those who are sexually free will exist in a kind of orgiastic anarchy. Overall those in sexually free cultures are no more or less sexually active than those who live in a sexually oppressed civilization. The frequency of sexual activity is not the main concern here. One can be sexually active and still oppressed. The difference is to be found in basic values. The islanders value sex as natural, beautiful, and good. It is something to be enjoyed—to add to the richness of life. Aboriginal people are pro-life. Westerners coming out of the Christian tradition view sex as sinful. Even if one personally disagrees with this anti-sex view, as many do these days, the culture exists within an anti-life historical context that unconsciously influences popular social values.

This anti-sex attitude extends itself to include misogyny and ecocide. It has so distorted primal values as to call the position against a women's right over her body as "pro-life." The anti-abortion position of the Christian Right is not about pro-life, it is about anti-sex

8   Malinowski, *The Sexual Life of Savages*. 54-56

and control over women. The history behind the Church oppressing women's rights over their own bodies includes the Inquisition when Christians tortured and murdered several hundred thousands of women. At about this time the modern university was born, and along with it came the then all male dominated medical school. The older kind of medicine was grounded in the paganism of pre-Christian culture wherewith the women with their knowledge of healing herbs doctored the sick. One of the services of these women was midwifery, which included if need be, abortions. The patriarchy of the Church outlawed midwifery and all other forms of medicine not regulated by the state, giving authority for such over to the university educated male doctors.

Christianity as Platonism for the masses carries with it the anti-organic presuppositions inherited from Platonic metaphysics. Plato's divided and ascending lines are metaphors for neurosis. The divided line fragments the psyche into libido and intellect. The ascending line is the symbol of the act of repressing libido and sublimating its energy into intellectual abstractions. Civilization is built on the sublimation of sexual energy into the labor of political economy. This dynamic creates alienated individuals, split off from the flow of the Way, and produces in them an artificially separated ego set apart from and in conflict with Nature. Moreover this alienated ego exists in the context of war. It is produced in struggle against sexual energy and Nature. The essence of its existence is anti-life. Socially this yields an inter-personal environment in which each person is isolated from and in competition with every other person. This is an environment of low-synergy. The ethno-psychology of aboriginal people is high-synergy. A high-synergy society is one in which there is no alienation and there exists an abundance of social togetherness. In high-synergy culture people live and work with each other so as to make life good for everyone.

Capitalism by its very nature is low-synergy. In a capitalistic society some few individuals win at the expense of others' loss. Capitalism is about "looking out for number one" in a power struggle against all competitors. In it wealth is concentrated into the hands of the few whereas the majority is left with little and many live in poverty. In high-synergy culture wealth tends to get spread around. In aboriginal tribes individualism as we know it in the West does not exist. Identity is diffused throughout the community, wherein one identifies oneself in relationship to family, clan, tribe, and ecological space. The result of this is that high-synergy culture tends to be non-aggressive and highly cooperative. People work together for the common good, and the common good is not different from the good of each person. By contrast civilization is about force, violence, competing, hording, and the like. The high-synergy of aboriginal culture is about togetherness and sharing, wherein each person's happiness is related to the happiness of all. Such an environment, asserts Margaret Mead, is easy to grow up in. She writes:

"The Samoan background which makes growing up so easy, so simple a matter, is the general casualness of the whole society. For Samoa is a place where no one plays for very high stakes, no one pays very heavy prices, no one suffers for his convictions or fights to the death for special ends. Disagreements between parent and child are settled by the child's moving across the street, between a man and his village by the man's removal to the next village, between a husband and his wife's seducer by a few fine mats. Neither poverty nor great disasters threaten the people to make them hold their lives dearly and tremble for continued existence. No implacable gods, swift to anger and strong to punish . . . No one is hurried along in life or punished harshly for slowness of development. Instead the gifted, the precocious, are held back, until the slowest among them have caught the pace. And in personal relations, caring is as slight. Love and hate, jealousy and revenge, sorrow and bereavement, are all matters of weeks. From the first months of life, when the child is handed carelessly from one women's hands to another's the lesson is learned of not caring for one person greatly, not setting high hopes on any one relationship." [9]

Mead wrote of diffusion of emotional relationships as one attribute that makes the Samoan culture healthy. What this means is that no one is overly attached to any one person. Rather feelings are diffused throughout many people in the community. In village life everybody is related by family to everyone else. A child is not raised by a mother alone, but by all the people of the extended family and the whole village. If a child finds difficulty with someone in the

---

[9]   Mead, *Coming of age in Samoa.* 110

household, she or he is free to move out and live with whomever she or he pleases. And children are welcome almost any place. I found it not all that easy to figure out which kids were the offspring of which parents as they just moved together as a pack from household to household, eating together, playing together and sleeping wherever they just so happen to be as it became night. They did not depend on just a few individuals for support as people do in the West, but were supported by the whole community.

Mead noted that in Samoa there are no Electra or Oedipus complexes. This is because no one becomes as attached to her or his biological mother or father as do children in Western culture. Freud over-generalized using too small a sample group to define the whole of humanity. It may be true that people raised in the West have Oedipus or Electra complexes, but it is not true of the whole of humanity, and it is not a natural condition of the psyche, but an artificial construct caused by a neurosis-producing Orestes project.

Wilhelm Reich argued that the authoritarian nuclear family structure is the principle means through which historically inherited neuroses are transmitted. It provides the social environment for the formation of Oedipus and Electra complexes while holding the child prisoner to anti-life indoctrination. In Samoa, as in other indigenous cultures, children are free from authoritarian restriction. The children move about with playful freedom, never being punished, but at the same time held responsible for their own behavior as equals to adults as much as maturity would allow. There are not two standards, but one as there is but one community, and everybody irrespective of age but according to ability is responsible for their own behavior. Mead writes:

"The next great difference between Samoa and our [Western] culture which may be credited with a lower production of maladjusted individuals is the difference in attitudes toward sex and the education of children in matters pertaining to birth and death. None of the facts of sex or birth are regarded as unfit for children, no child has to conceal its knowledge for fear of punishment or ponder painfully over little understood occurrences."[10]

_____

[10]   Mead, *Coming of Age in Samoa.* 120

The customary dwellings in Samoa are typically one-room open-air structures. Living in an extended family in such a dwelling means that privacy is practically impossible. Every child has witnessed sex acts multiple times long before entering puberty. Although Samoans are not exhibitionistic, they are not traditionally very shy over sexual matters. I recall a visit to a remote village during which I stayed for a few days with a Samoan family who had an electric generator, a television, and a video player. For my entertainment, they gathered together the extended family, from young children to grandparents, and put into the video player a pornographic video for everyone to view. There was no thought that pornography ought not to be viewed by children, or that it is not appropriate for family entertainment. Actually, they had very little interest in pornography. Why should they? They are not sexually repressed. I asked my host why he chose this for the occasion. He said, "Is this not the kind of stuff that Papalagi like?" He told me he got the video out of curiosity about Papalagi society. There is little to no interest among Samoans for sexually explicit entertainment. Sexual life in Samoa is rich enough that they would not find much value, beyond passing curiosity, in pornography. Indeed the obsession over pornography in the West is symptomatic of a psychological deficiency rooted in misogyny. In a culture in which women are respected and sex is not repressed, pornography has little value.

On a different occasion with a different Samoan family with whom I was socializing, there was a prepubescent boy playing about in the nude, as is not uncommon for children his age in island cultures. At one point he got an erection and started to masturbate. No one thought anything of it and nothing was said. In a Western family the boy would probably have been punished, or at the very least told not to do that. Mead reports that Samoan boys sometimes masturbate in groups. It just is not regarded as wrong. And why should it be?—It gives pleasure and harms no one.

The act of giving birth is a social event in which the people of the village gather to witness the birthing. Thus children do not have to wonder where babies come from, they know through direct observation. Also death is not hidden. Every child knows death in the same way that she or he knows birth. When relatives are dying, they are not isolated from the family, rather everyone gathers around the dying person to give each other emotional support. Birth and death are natural parts of life, and are accepted as such, whereas in the West for the most part we segregate these events from our lives and often go about as if they do not even exist. In Samoa the dead relatives are often buried on the grounds of the home, and children will play on and around the graves. It is not seen as morbid. Western children are "protected" from the facts of sex, birth, and death. This increases the likelihood that when the child does encounter one of these experiences, the child may be traumatized—especially if the child picks up on the highly negative cultural attitudes that are associated with such, as she or he is likely to do.

Wilhelm Reich refers to authoritarian patriarchal civilization as existing within an "emotional plague." James DeMeo, a follower of Reich, did his doctoral research on a detailed mapping of the diffusion of this plague from it geographic origins in central Asia to throughout Eurasia and North Africa and beyond to just about the whole planet. In his book, *Saharasia,* DeMeo points out that before this plague, which begins about six thousand years ago, cultures the world over were mostly peaceful. Supporting this position is the archeological evidence gathered together by Marija Gimbutas and confirmed by others clearly showing that prior to the advent of patriarchy, there is no significant evidence of much warfare. Also absent are socio-political divisions in which one class oppresses and rules over others. In fact there was no class structure to these early cultures. These early cultures were overrun by people whose social organization was military, and whose form of economics was the conquest, subjugation and enslavement of the people whose lands they invaded. Patterns of social behavior that DeMeo accounts for originating with patriarchy includes ritual body deformation, genital mutilation, high bride price, patrilineal descent with property right thereof, authoritarian family organization dominated by husbands, slavery, sexual exploitation, rape, and other forms of sex violence against women, and other kinds of related acts and conditions. The closer to the Indo-European homeland the more common these patterns are, whereas the farther away from thus the less common said patterns are; and one can map out the historical diffusion of these traits from their geographic origins. On the peripheral of the areas of greatest intensity some of these patterns made way into

Oceania and the Americas, but one also finds a greater number of matrilineal cultures not so affected with an absence of these patterns prior to modernity with significant exceptions being the Mayas, Incas and Aztecs and a few other cultures whose histories exist within the last two thousand years and for which evidence exists that these are related to influences coming from Eurasian origins.

Many of these patterns persist into modern times most intensely in societies that are most rigidly patriarchal. For example, some Muslim dominated African communities carry out a very cruel and painful rite of genital mutilation on young girls. In this "female circumcision" the clitoris is cut out or removed. There may be further mutilation or removal of external female genitalia. The result, apart from pain and risk of infection, is loss of capacity for sexual pleasure. Also in some Muslim communities in the Middle East there is a practice of killing girls who have pre-marital sex, and it is their own families who are duty bound to do this, more often than not by the fathers or brothers. This is a practice that has its grounding and justification in the Hebrew Torah, which also allows fathers to sell their own daughters into slavery.

The treatment of women as property is a common trait of patriarchy and central to the historical nature of marriage in civil ethos. The pattern established by the Indo-Europeans and adapted by those influenced by them was that for a man to gain a wife he must pay the woman's father for the right to marriage subject to the will and consent of the father, and once married the women was duty bound to submit and obey her husband. This is part of the reason for the custom of killing girls who have sex before marriage—in doing so they have lost economic value as potential wives.

Another wide spread practice ranging from the Vikings to India is widow killing. It was the custom in those societies that upon the death of the husband the wife would be sacrificed to him. This practice continued into modern times in India where it was the responsibility of the elder son to see to it that his own mother was ritually killed. We thus have a ritual enactment of the Orestes Project where the son kills his own mother as a patriarchal duty. This symbolizes the essence of patriarchy.

A problem with DeMeo's work however is his views on homosexuality. Reich agreed with Freud that homosexuality is symptomatic of a psychological disorder. Influenced by this view DeMeo asserts that homosexuality is unnatural, and that it is caused by socio-environmental factors historically originating with patriarchy. He further asserts that it was not present to any significant degree in pre-patriarchal cultures, and it is not to be found in animal behavior among animals living in the wild. The truth is opposite of these assertions.

To begin with consider the sex life of bonobos, who along with chimpanzees are the primates most closely related to humans. They are perhaps the most sexually active primates with high frequency of multiple partners both male and female. Bisexuality is clearly the social norm among bonobos, and this is likewise true of all primates. Moreover homoerotic behavior has been observed in most mammal spices in the wild as documented by biologists like Bruce Bagemihl and Volker Sommer. Therefore to the extent that anything can be called natural, homosexual behavior must be. In this context it would seem very odd that what is common among all other primates and most mammals should not be the case for humans, and indeed the preponderance of evidence indicates that homosexuality exist in all human societies. The Kinsey Institute for Research in Sex, Gender, and Reproduction at Indiana University provides evidence that most people cross-culturally will at some time in their lives participate in homoerotic behavior even if they otherwise at other times prefer heterosexual relationships, and that about ten percent of any given population has an overall homosexual preference. Research also shows that no theory of socio-environmental causality for homosexual behavior has predictive validity, and thus those theories cannot be held as scientifically true. At the same time some evidence indicates that there may be a biological basis for sexual orientation.[11]

As for the assertion that non-patriarchal societies do not have homosexuality, all one needs to prove this false is to look at the evidence provided by anthropologists like Water Williams and Will Roscoe, among others, whose studies have focused on homoerotic behavior among indigenous tribes, the very cultures that DeMeo identified as sex-positive. There is also the work of Paula Gunn Allen, an American Indian lesbian who argued that traditional Indian cultures

---

[11]   Bell. Weinberg, Hammersmith, *Sexual Preference*

are homoerotic friendly, and points out that it is the European based societies that have been violently homophobic. Part of the reason that most early anthropologists did not discover homosexuality among indigenous people is that as the tribes encountered the Westerners, they experience their extreme violence toward homosexual behavior, and thus learned to hide it from them. It was not until openly gay and lesbian anthropologists came into the field that the tribal people opened up and allowed the truth to be known. Over all it is patriarchy that produces problems with its unnatural rejection of homosexuality. It is the natural way for each person to be free to follow whatever her or his spontaneous sexual pleasures may be.

Humanity under the domination of patriarchy is so conditioned by anti-life indoctrination as to fear organic reality, and so acquires "pleasure anxiety." This produces a deficiency psychology—living in endless desire and never knowing fullness. Reich refers to this as "armoring," which happens with people whose sexual impulses are sublimated into a psychological character structure that is harsh and brutal. The soft and gentle quality of life becomes lost, and the person is unable to feel any fullness of pleasure, indeed she or he learns to fear such gratification associating it with loss of control and ego death. Organic gratification is replaced by artificiality, and desire becomes about such things as ego status, public persona, ownership of property and other such things that have no natural grounding. No amount of attaining to these artificially generated desires can bring about a feeling of fullness. Taoism asserts that desire end with the tranquility of harmony with the Way. In the emotional plague one struggles against nature, and thus lives in disharmony. The basic energy of life thus becomes out of balance and does not flow naturally.

Much of the origins of this problem come from sex being associated with sin. This anti-life notion of "sin" deprives much of humanity of the ability to enjoy sex, and such makes them more predisposed to be violent. James Prescott for his part writes, "Violence against sexuality and the use of sexuality for violence, particularly against women, has very deep roots in Biblical tradition." Much of what one finds in the religions of the Western world is anti-sex and thus anti-life. By contrast indigenous religions are sin free and one with that which is Natural. One may see this in the following from *For Every North American Indian:*

"The European was born in sin. Dammed at birth. He felt and knew the burden of his guilt before he was three years of age—and carried it, in fear and trembling, throughout a life punctuated with condemnation and confession. His church was furnished with replicas of dead martyrs and crucified Christs. The principle religious observances were heavy with death. Nor was the adherent himself encouraged to live fully and openly, to laugh and be joyous; rather he was instructed to endure life in sinless obedience and to hope and pray and yearn and seek after salvation.

"The Indian was born into and blessed by life. He was guilt free, (which infuriated Europeans) and had no 'conscience,' as such. His standards of conduct and responsibility were set by a tradition of dignity, mutual respect and generosity. If his conduct fell below recognized standards, he lost face—his tribal stature shrank to a dimension appropriate to his behavior. He was expected to live fully, openly and happily. His church was the out-of-doors and most of his activities were sacraments which demonstrated a consistent reverence for life and gratitude for supply. His religious ceremonies were either supplications or celebrations of life. Psychologically, he sought nothing. He had what the Europeans hope and prayed for." [12]

There are thousands of religions among the many peoples of the world. Among the America Indians alone there are many hundreds distributed among the many tribes. Most of these religions may have a few hundred to a few thousand adherents. And they are geographically defined to function within a particular ecology in accordance to gynocentric values. The religions that have followers in the many millions are relatively few and patriarchal in values and structure. Also, the biggest among them are so called 'world religions,' which belong to no place in particular. The world religions can be taken into outer space, but the indigenous religions cannot be removed from the place of origins without significant modification and reintroduction into some ecological place. Primal mythos always belongs to a place. Patriarchal mythology is on a linear time-line always in the process of departing from place to place. These religions in their orthodox forms

---

[12]   Pelletier, *For Every North American Indian*. 32-33

assert that this world is a place of suffering, and salvation consists of overcoming the world and the physical body. In the religions that come out of historical India this world is thought of as like a wheel of life, death, and rebirth, and the aim is to break out. Here is a metaphor of the broken Circle, which symbolizes the patriarchal break with the life-affirming religions of primal people. Yes, there is suffering in this world, but most of it is self inflicted or socially induced. Given a healthy way of living, this life can be a source of joy, happiness, pleasure, and beauty. Primal reality is one with the Wheel—the whole Wheel—and the Wheel is the womb of life. Being one with the Medicine Wheel requires unity of mind, body, and spirit.

In the theology of monotheism matter and spirit is set apart, but in primal spirituality the materiality of Nature is alive with spirit. Such it is that among aboriginal religions spirituality is found in Deep Ecology. The religions that inform modern society are ones in which nature is fallen and in need of conquest. The people who follow the old ways are likewise in need of conquest, and this in turn leads to genocide and destruction of the natural world. Nietzsche said that Christianity is Platonism for the masses, a view which is an echo of a similar sentiment in Hegel. In essence what is suggested in Platonism is that the world of the body, that is to say the organic world, is of no real value; what is of true value is abstract and of the mind.

With modernity the world was conceived as being a machine, and god was like an engineer who created the world as an artifact, then removed himself from it to allow it to run according to preset laws. Modern science has for all practical purposes divorced itself from any notion of the divine and reduced life to a materialistic determinism in which everything is made of dumb and lifeless stuff being pushed about by blind and impersonal laws. Thus it is that modernity kills God! And nothing is sacred! Existence is thus absurd and life is meaningless. Nihilism is at the core of modernity. Jean Paul Sartre said that Nature is mute. Nature is an 'it'—something that may be used for consumption without any intrinsic value apart from man-centric use. This is the opposite position of aboriginal religions. Nature to aboriginals is personal; she is a 'thou!' One can be in communion with her. She is sacred! And life is full of meaning! Lao-tzu likewise said that Nature is sacred, and warns us that if we try to improve on her we will spoil Nature.

The pathology of civilization most intensified in modernity is related to the loss of the sense of natural sacredness. Civil ethos has parted with the Way. Prior to modernity the place of greatest intensity of socio-pathology was Europe. The further away one moved from Europe, the less intense was this pathology—the closer to European centers of power the more violence and political oppression one historically finds. With the European invasion of America and the genocide that followed, the United States became the culmination of socio-pathology, raping the earth more diligently than all previous societies in history combined. Holmes Welch speculates on what Lao-tzu would say about the dominant culture of the United States and writes this:

"America's greatest troubles come from the advertising business . . . . It makes people want to buy things that they would not otherwise want to buy. It fills their minds with desires for ingenious devices and with ambition to have more than their neighbors. How, confused by ingenuity, can their character become simple? On the contrary, they must be always excessively active to earn the money to buy what has been produced by the excessive activity of others . . . The next of your great troubles is education . . . Your American college is a school of struggle. Examinations are struggle, athletics are struggle, fraternities are struggle. Instead of teaching a boy to unlearn all the vicious competitive ways he has acquired from childhood, it reinforces them. Instead of turning his mind inwards, it fills him with ambition. Instead of making him quiet and opening his ears to intuitive understanding, it disturbs him and stifles his inner powers . . . What else could be expected? The teachers—the very ones who should be healing young minds sick with struggle—are sick themselves. Like creaking champions they have to be ever padding themselves with heavier degrees and the production of thicker books, straining their ears for faculty rumor, sharpening their tongues for cleverness and reprisal . . . I have just spoken of the danger of college sports. All sports are dangerous. Could anything destroy character more surely? Sometimes you call sport a 'harmless substitutes' for warfare. Sometimes you make it part of military training. Sometimes the individual participates with his own body and sometimes by watching others. But always the result is the same. He learns to expect success by force. He learns to think of himself habitually as part of one group against another group. He tastes the fruits of victory and the weeds of defeat—more dangerous than opium . . . Defeat and victory: these are the terms in which you Americans think of almost everything you do, and so it is impossible for you to do anything without it recoiling upon you. What is there that you have not made into a struggle? Your political elections are a struggle between two parties; your careers are a struggle to get ahead of fellow workers. Consider the Social Register, the Critics' Awards, the Miss. America Contest, the Kentucky Derby, the National Spelling bee—everywhere I see struggle. But all this makes you beam with pleasure and knock your heads three times in homage to the 'fair free competition' which you say, has made America succeed. I say to you, your success is failure and your competition drives half your people mad with praise while it drives the other half mad with blame . . ." [13]

In the modern world, we are fragmented, both socially and psychologically. This gives us a low-synergy society in which there is little or no sense of community. A result of Euro-American competitiveness is that one's success is at the expense of others. In the greatest of social synergy, no one wins if anyone losses. If any member of the community is hungry, homeless, sick, unhappy, or the like, it is of concern to the whole society. Wealth is not personal, but social. In a high-synergy culture wealth exists for the good of all. High-synergy manifests when people live in harmony with the Way. The Way is cultivated in the lives of the people when the mind is quiet and the spirit comes to center.

---

[13]   Welch, Taoism: the Parting of the Way. 54-56

THE WAY OF THE CENTER: BEING WHOLE

Ch'i as the basic energy of the universe is the stuff out of which life manifests. When ch'i manifests it divides into yin and yang. Everything in Nature has yin and yang. Harmony with the Way depends on the balance of these two. This balance is the harmony of male and female. It is the loving embrace of opposites that produces life. When they are not in harmony sickness follows. The Native American philosophy of the Sacred Hoop and Taoist metaphysics agree on this. Jimmie Begay of the Navajo writes the following on the philosophy of his People:

"Each animal, each plant has a place in the Universe. And every living thing needs both female and male aspects to work together, to create growth. The human is a special creation placed on Earth to do certain things. Each person has his own practice in our religion—male or female. Everyone has some power, some knowledge, some wisdom. The Earth and Sky are teachers for everyone.

"In human, 50 per cent of us is the female force, and 50 per cent is the male force. It is important to keep these in balance. If the female side or the male side takes over completely, then you are out of balance, and you need a ceremony to be done for you to put you back in harmony with the Universe.

"I understand that scientists and psychologists are now working on what they call 'right brain or left brain dominance.' They have discovered that the right side of the brain controls the left side of the body, and that the left brain controls the right side of each human being. They have discovered through scientific experiments that contemporary American children have not developed the right brain to the same degree as Indian children. They find in contemporary Americans a 'left-brain dominance'—what we Navajos would call an unbalance toward the male power. The female side of the contemporary American brain is not developed, and rarely used. That means that all of the contemporary American society is out of balance with nature, using only half of the power that was given to them by the Great Spirit." [14]

The up-and-to-the-right orientation—frontal lobes of the left-brain—is causing us to be out of balance with Nature. This is due to the priority that reason is given as a tool to conquer Nature. According to the teachings of the Medicine Wheel, the four modes must harmonize for there to be health. The North and South work with each other, as do the East and West. The North is thinking, which is the priority of civil ethos. The South is feeling, which is the anti-priority of civilization. Civil humanity has thus become emotionally retarded. The hyper-yang priority of reason is the root of the emotional plague. Feelings are treated as a threatening enemy of the civilized mind. In the philosophy of Great Harmony, being in touch with feelings is very important. On the importance of feelings in Indian culture Wilfred Pelletier said this:

"Your history books say that when the White men first came here they noted that the Indians were very child-like. That is very true in many ways. But if you look at it, how beautiful to be child-like and yet be mature. Here [in white society] we say you mustn't show feelings. I don't agree with that. If a man can cry, then he has feelings. Indians cry all the time. We get together and sing songs and we cry in these songs. But this [Western] society is very machine-like, and so we begin to act like machines and then we become machines." [15]

Thinking that is out of touch with feeling is machine-like. This thinking-centered sickness is as a weapon in a war against Nature. Modern technology is thus produced. Aboriginal people live in harmony with the Way, but the war machine has moved us out of harmony with Nature. This fall from harmony began with the patriarchal conquest of gynocentric cultures. The war chariot has spread patriarchy like a cancerous growth—conquering and destroying as it goes! The essence of civilization is war.

Lao-tzu taught that to live a violent life is to die an unnatural death—much like the saying "He who lives by the sword will die by

---

[14] Begay, "Nature: The core of Navajo Religion," Navajo Times, May 31, 1979

[15] Pelletier, *Two Articles*

the sword." Francis Bacon describes the scientific method in terms of placing Mother Earth on the rack and torturing her for her secrets. Bacon's social vision was that of conquering and controlling Nature, and the metaphors he used were derived from the Inquisition. He gave us the philosophy of technology, the essence of which is the Orestes Project. Modernity is the most violent social phenomena ever! The reality of this situation is suicidal! The question then is what can be done?

Conventional psychology in the service of the state aims at behavioral modification and adaptation of maladapted individuals so as to bring them into line with socially defined norms. If you had been living in Nazi Germany and not adapting well to those social norms, then it would have been the job of the psychologist to make you a good Nazi. In nineteenth century Euro-American society if you were a woman who was disobedient to the will of your husband, he was empowered by the law and the norms of that culture to force you into a surgical treatment involving the mutilation of your sex organ, which was supposed to cure you of your infliction, as if resistance to oppression was abnormal. The Women's Movement is a natural reaction to patriarchal oppression. By a standard of normality that is transcultural and grounded in Nature those that are maladapted to the social norm of a pathological society may be the ones who are healthiest. In a high-synergy culture there is no oppression, and people are free to follow their nature. In low-synergy societies there is a great deal of oppression, and individuals are forced into conformity. If anyone behaves inconsistently with these artificially constructed norms, then she or he is dealt with harshly.

In ancient China when something of the old culture still survived at the level of the peasant village and a few people in the educated aristocracy took note of this in contrast to the ever-intensifying violence that was erupting all around them, they realized that these old ways were much more benevolent than those being produced by the political state. Some of these few chose to drop-out and head to the hills. Lao-tzu was one of them, and another was Yang Chu. The critics of Yang Chu characterized him as a selfish hedonist. Yang Chu taught that if each person truly remained in touch with organic pleasures as can be had through the care and love of one's body, then one would not indulge in modes of activity that would compromise one's happiness. If the whole society were like that then civil politics would end, resulting in a return to the original state of benevolence. The problem with the political state is that the ruling class interferes too much in the lives of the people. If you contribute to the system as such, you become part of the problem—not only that but you compromise the quality of your own life. Thus if you are in-tune with your own well-being then you will not do those things that disrupt the quality of life for yourself and others. In the Taoist vision of the old ways people did not impose on one another, and lived in accordance with inborn nature. *The Book of Lieh-tzu* in the chapter of Yang Chu, reads:

"The men of the distant past know that in life we are here for a moment and in death we are gone for a moment. Therefore they acted as their hearts prompted, and did not rebel against their spontaneous desires; while life lasted they did not refuse its pleasures, and so they were not seduced by the hope of reputation. They roamed as their nature prompted, and did not rebel against the desires common to things; they did not prefer a reputation after death, and so punishment did not affect them. Whether they were reputed and praised more or less than others, whether their destined years were many or few, they did not take into account." [16]

We do not have any original writings of Yang Chu. Everything we know about him is from accounts from others. The historical record said of him that he was a man who would not pluck out of his body a single hair even if it would benefit the world, and he similarly would not do so to gain the world. For the Confucianist this was evidence that he was a very selfish man and socially unethical. It is the duty, taught Confucian ethics, to do that which benefits society even at ones own personal expense. From Yang Chu's point of view the very political state that the Confucian philosophy is preserving and perpetuating is the very source of the problem. The notion of ethical duty in which people are willing to compromise their heath and well-being is what leads to the violence of the dominant society. If every one were to be sensitive to one's own health and well-being, and enjoy the pleasures of the body, then the pathology of the political state would end. His critics call him a hedonist, but he was not so in the sense of materialistic

---

[16]   Graham, The Book of Lieh-tzu. 140

gluttony. He was in fact a minimalist. He advocated finding pleasure in the simplest of things and not troubling one's well-being with the activity of accumulating things and the anxiety of holding to them. The problem with a consumption mode of hedonism is that much of one's time is taken up by doing things one does not really want to do in order to get the wealth that one wants, and when thus gotten it does not lead to much real satisfaction but results in a life of discontent. Consumer materialism is an addiction, and lacking the wisdom to see the insanity of the predicament, much less an alternative, keeps one running on the same old treadmill somehow expecting that it may in the long run lead to a different result.

If possession of things means placing one's life or health in danger, then having things is not worth it. Yang Chu gave health and well-being priority over wealth and social status. Placing one's body or heath in danger in order to gain something artificial and abstract is insane, but that is what most of us are doing day in and day out. It has become known that most heart attacks happen within the time of morning rush hours, and then mostly on Mondays. It is also well known that most people do not like their jobs, and feel trapped into them by economic condition that rob them of the joy of living. Everyone is also aware of the lies, deception and corruption of the politicians. Those who govern perpetuate insanity, and they do this out of insensitivity to their own biological well-being and the insensitivity to the suffering of those whom they govern—indeed they significantly add to the pain. Lao-tzu asserted that governing ought to be trusted to those who are sensitive to the well being of their bodies and able to extend that to others:

> "Of fame and body, which is dearer?
> Of body and property, which is worth more?
> Of gain and loss, which is more troublesome? . . .
>
> Big trouble should be treated as seriously as our bodies.
> What is meant by, 'Favor is like disgrace, which startle us?'
> Favor is lowly.
> Getting it startles us;
> Losing it startles us;
> Thus favor is like disgrace, which startles us.

What is meant by, 'Big troubles are treated as seriously as
our bodies?'
The reason that we have big troubles is that we possess
bodies.
If we did not possess bodies, what troubles could we have?
Therefore, only the man who values himself for the sake of
the world is worthy of being entrusted with the world.
Only the man who loves himself for the sake of the world is
worthy of being relied on by the world." [1]

In *Chuang-tzu* there is a study of two political states at war over
a piece of territory. The warlord of one side was becoming very
concern that things would not turn out well. He asked advice from
a Taoist sage. The sage gave him a hypothetical situation, "Now
imagine that the people of the world were to present you with a
document which read, 'If you lay hold of this with your left hand,
you will lose your right hand; lay hold with your right hand, and you
will lose your left hand; however, if you lay hold of this, you will also
rule the world'" The warlord said he would not lay hold of it at all.
The sage went on to say, "From that point of view, I can certainly
see that your two hands are more important than the whole world.
Furthermore, your body itself is more important than just your two
hands. The whole of [your state of] Han is much less important than
the whole of the world and this scrap of land you are fighting over is
of less significance than Han . . . if you so value your body and your
life, you should not be following a path of misery and distress trying
to seize this territory."[2]

In the classic Taoists text *Han-fei-tzu*, Yang Chu is described as
someone who would not place himself in danger, would not serve in
the military, and would not do anything that would gain him great
profit even if it would coast him only one hair from his body. He lived
out in wilderness away from the centers of civil activity. He and others
like him did not drop-out as an act of irresponsibility; rather they did
so as a means to preserve their virtue and to avoid contamination
from the pathology of disharmony. By being of no use to a sick society

---

[1] Wu, *The Book of Lao-tzu*, Chapters 13 and 44
[2] Palmer, *The Book of Chuang Tzu*. 251

and yet remaining within social consciousness one serves the end of healthiness for the culture. This is the Taoist teaching of the utility of no utility. It is similar to the position of Virginia Woolf who argued that women ought not to contribute to patriarchal civilization, for to do so is to work against one's own best interests by helping that which is against women. Indeed patriarchy is against life, thus anyone who works for it works against life. By being useful to a life destroying system one destroys one's own life.

In *Chuang-tzu* a story is told of a meeting between Lao-tzu and Confucius. In this story Confucius went to see Lao-tzu to speak with him about moral philosophy. Lao-tzu asked him if he thought that morality was innate. Confucian philosophy does hold that human nature is basically good, and on this Lao-tzu agreed. It was Mencius who nearly two hundred years after Confucius gave explicit articulation to the Confucian notion that human nature is innately good. He argued that no normal healthy human being could bear to see another suffer. To illustrate his point he said that if anyone sees a child about to fall into a well, it would be natural to respond with feelings of alarm and distress. Mencius argued for what David Hume would come to think of as a moral sentiment. It was Hume who called into question the long-standing tradition in the West that placed morality in the domain of reason over and against passions and emotions. In what is now known as the "naturalistic fallacy" he pointed out that one cannot get an "ought" out of "is"—that reason can clarify the nature of facts, but facts cannot inform values, and they can not tell what is right to do. Values come out of feelings and the emotions. In Chinese philosophy this was known from ancient times, and so ethical theories among the Chinese always accented feelings like empathy, loyalty, and love.

Sociobiologist Marc Hauser has done empirical research that gives strong evidence to support the position that there is a universal biologically based moral sentiment. He has surveyed thousands of individuals from varieties of different backgrounds asking them to respond to hypothetical simulations that call for making moral choices. His findings are that most people agree on what the right thing to do is, and that there is no statistically significant difference with regard to ethnicity, religion, language, education, geography and other types of differences between peoples. He suggests that the moral sense may be like what Noam Chomsky called "deep grammar," which is to say that our capacity to learn language is innate and that there is a fundamental structure to all languages that makes them more similar than not. So also there is a fundamental sentimentality to morality, so that Mencius' baby falling into a well is likely to facilitate a common response with all biological normal humans. Hauser wrote, "that the universality stems from our shared capacity not only to experience emotions, but to experience the same sort of emotions in certain contexts. The reason why everyone would find it morally abhorrent to watch or imagine an adult kicking a helpless infant is that everyone would experience disgust in this context. Our shared emotional code generates a shared moral code." [3]

The big question here is why people do bad things? The short answer is that it is a deficiency disease, like a deformity from lack of proper nutrients. The organic perspective of Chinese philosophy has it that just as a plant needs nutrient rich soil, warmth, water and sunlight to grow, any lack of these benefits will result in lack of proper growth. In like manner a child has needs both physical and emotional, including love, affection, stimulation, play, friendly social interaction and the like. Oftentimes when one looks into the personal histories of sociopaths, or those who have committed hideous crimes, one finds a dysfunctional and abusive up-bringing in which basic needs were not filled. Our social environment imprints itself upon us and we in turn tend to replicate that imprinting into our offspring. The home environment of the child is the primary locus of moral cultivation, and it has become in the civilized world pathological. It was Lao-tzu position that Confucius was inadvertently advocating a political philosophy that would not solve the problem, but compound it.

Confucius asserted that patriarchy is natural. In agreement with Aristotle, he argued that it is proper and natural that men rule and women submit to the domination of their husbands. The state was conceived to be like a family with the ruler being akin to the husband, and the people his children in that they were to submit to his authority and obey him. This is not how cultures that are in harmony with Nature function. Confucius was thus advocating a moral education

---

[3]   Hauser, *Moral Minds.* 44

that would fit a person into a social environment that goes against Nature and as such perverts the natural moral sentiment. What is natural does not need to be imposed from the outside; it only needs to be allowed to grow from the inside. All forms of indoctrination are antithetical to moral growth. In *Chuang-tzu,* Loa-tzu is attributed to having said to Confucius:

"Heaven and earth hold fast to their constant ways, the sun and the moon to their brightness, the stars and planets to their rank, the birds and beast to their flocks, the trees and shrubs to their stands. You have only to go along with Virtue in your action, to follow the Way in your journey, and already you will be there. Why these flags of benevolence and righteousness so bravely upraised, as though you were beating a drum and searching for a lost child? Ah, you will bring confusion to the nature of [hu]man[ity] . . . .

"The snow goose needs no daily bath to stay white; the crow needs no daily inking to stay black. Black and white in their simplicity offer no ground for argument; fame and reputation in their clamorousness offer no ground for envy. When the spring dries up and the fish are left stranded on the ground, they spew each other with moisture and wet each other down with spit—but it would be much better if they could forget each other in the rivers and lakes!" [4]

By analogy, the spring began to dry up some six thousand years ago, and has dried up all the more so in the last few hundred years. Artificial morality is as "spew[ing]" and "spit[ing]." Humanity in the gynocentric pre-history, "could forget each other." Virtue is innate and thus needs "no daily bath." When the spirit is free, behavior is good; if effort is made to be good, failure results. Goodness comes forth out of innate virtue through effortless action. Virtue is that which follows Nature, which is to be in Great Harmony with the Way.

Confucius represents patriarchy in Chinese civilization. Lao-tzu preserves the gynocentric. As much as they are opposed to each other, the difference between them is not as great as that between Taoism and the West. Both Lao-tzu and Confucius agree that virtue entails harmony with the Way; that human nature is basically good, and that life and Nature are beautiful and sacred. The closest mode of thought in ancient China to the dominant tradition of Western

---

[4]   Watson, *The Complete Works of Chuang Tzu.* 149 and 163

thought is Legalism, which asserts that human nature is bad and must be regulated through laws that are backed up by police and military force. China has throughout its history used legalistic principles, but morally condemns it. What the Confucian scholars seem to fail to see is that the seeds of Legalism are in the patriarchal traditions that Confucianism helps to preserve.

Philosophers from both East and West have argued over issues of right and wrong. Many competing views have been put forth, and none are adequate, indeed moralism has often made things bad. Some of what Marc Hauser's research has shown is that even when people can agree as to what is right and wrong, they disagree as to why. Often in our history moralist ideology has led humanity to commit acts of violence and partake in other activities that they 'know' are wrong but do it all the same even in the name of what they think to be "good." According to Taoism, moralism has not worked because it calls for action based on knowledge—and goodness is not and cannot be an object of knowledge. The Way as a normative wisdom moves beyond knowledge to the realm of freedom with Nature, in which virtue may spontaneously actualize without use of effort.

In *Chuang-tzu* there is a discourse on the problem of moral relativism and the way in which Taoism accommodate such. It is said that the Way is hidden by rhetoric, so that there is but partial understanding. What one school of thought asserts as right, another asserts as wrong, and what one asserts as wrong the other asserts as right. Everyone has a point of view that is her or his "this-ness" in contrast to others points of view, which is "that-ness." One cannot know others' point of view as one knows one's own. The "this-ness" is never experience by oneself as "that-ness," and "that-ness" is not experienced as "this-ness." Never-the-less they are related to one another. We are social animals living in culture with language that we have inherent from our relations to one another, and our value system is articulated in the context of our interpersonal relationships. Everything that is "this" is someone's "that," and all the "that" is someone's "this," and each has it own right and wrong. But the relational dynamic of the whole means that at some fundamental level there is no separation. To enter into this place of no-separation one must look beyond "this" and "that" and seeing beyond right and wrong. This Chuang-tzu calls the "still-point of the Way." The still-point is like the center of the circle that symbolizes the wholeness of Great Harmony. To enter into this "still point" one must transcend thoughts and simply Be as Nature would have one be "self-so." From this still-point Lao-tzu described himself living in accord with the Way, thus:

> "Transcend learning, there will be no sorrow.
> Between 'yes' and 'no,' what is the difference?
> Between 'good' and 'evil,' what is the distinction?
> What other people fear, I cannot but fear.
> Of wandering, there will be no end.
> Most people are busy coming and going
> As if enjoying a feast,
> As if ascending a tower in the springtime.
> I alone am unmoved, showing no sign,
> Like a baby who has not yet become a child;
> Weary, as if I have no home to return to.
> Most people have more than enough;
> I alone seem to be left out.
> My mind is like a fool's Chaotic, chaotic!
> Ordinary people are bright; I alone am dim.
> Ordinary people inspect (everything); I alone am obscurant,
> Indifferent as the sea, endless as a high wind.
> Most people are reasonable;
> I alone am stubborn and mean.
> I am different from others;
> I value being fed by the Mother." [5]

---

[5]   Wu, *The Book of Lao-tzu*, Chapter 20

Walter Robinson has a Ph.D in philosophy and religion from the California Institute of Integral Studies. He teaches philosophy at Indiana University—Purdue University at Indianapolis. His areas of scholarship are East Asian and American Indian philosophies, which forms the basis of his critique of Western Thought.

The etymology of the name "Robinson" shows that it has Celtic roots in reference to the pagan god "Robin Good-fellow," also known as Puck, whose festival is May-Day which involves drinking, singing and dancing around the May-Pole, a phallic symbol of the deity. As such the festival is a fertility rite. In the evening the people go out into the fields for orgiastic sex which is believed to help the crops grow. A numbers of pregnancies usually result. The boys thus born are given the honored title of "the sons of Robin," thus Robinson. The name "Walter" has old Germanic roots meaning "lord of the forest" which is akin to Puck. This is the precursor to the mythological motif of "Robin Hood" who in his original archaic form was an archetypal warrior of the old pagan forest dwelling culture that fought against the encroachment of civilization.

BIBLIOGRAPHY

Akwesasne. *Basic Call to Consciousness*. Akwesasne Notes, 1978.

Allen, Paula. *The Sacred Hoop*. Beacon Press, 1986.

Awiakta, Marilou. Selu: *Seeking the Corn-Mother's Wisdom*. Fulcrum Publishing, 1993.

Bagemihl, Bruce. *Biological Exuberance*. St. Martin's Press, 1999.

Begay, Jimmie. "Nature: The Core of Navajo Religion." Navajo Times, May 31. 1979.

Bell, Alan, Weinberg, Martin, and Hammersmith, Sue. *Sexual Preference*. Olympic Marketing Corp. 1988.

Benedict, Ruth. *Patterns of Culture*. Houghton Mifflin, 1961.

Boyd, William. *The Emile of Jean Jacques Rousseau*. Columbia University, 1959.

Chan, Wing-tsit. *A Source Book in Chinese Philosophy*. Princeton University Press. 1963.

Commoner, Barry. *The Closing Circle*. Bantam Books, 1971.

Daily, Mary. *Gyn/Ecology*. Beacon Press, 1978.

Deloria, Vine Jr *God is Red*. Delta Books, 1973.

Demeo, James. *On the Origin and Diffusion of Patrism.* University of Kansas Ph.D. dissertation, 1986.

Eisler, Riane. *The Chalice and the Blade.* Harper and Row 1988.

Erdoes, Richard. *Lame Deer: Seeker of Visions.* Pocket Books, 1972.

Erdoes, Richard. *Crow Dog: Four Generations of Sioux Medicine Men.* HarperCollins 1995.

Feng, Gia-fu. and English, Jane. *Chuang Tsu: Inner Chapters.* Vintage Books, 1974.

Feng, Gia-fu. and English, Jane. *Lao tsu: Tao Te Ching.* Vintage Books, 1972.

Freud, Sigmund. *Civilization and Its Discontents.* Norton, 1961.

Freud, Sigmund. *The Ego and the Id.* Norton, 1960

Fung, Yu-lan. *History of Chinese Philosophy.* Princeton University Press, 1952

Gadon, Elinor. *The Once and Future Goddess.* Harper and Row, 1989.

Garrett, J.T. *The Cherokee Full Circle.* Bear and Company, 2002.

Gimbutas, Marija. *The Living Goddesses.* University of California Press, 1999.

Goodman, Paul. *Growing Up Absurd.* Vintage Books, 1956.

Graham, A.C. *The Book of Lieh-tzu.* Columbia University Press, 1960.

Hauser, Marc, *Moral Minds.* Ecco, 2006

Holmes, Lovell. *Quest for the Real Samoa.* Bergin and Garvey, 1987.

Jung, C.G. *Psychological Types.* Princeton University Press, 1971.

Jung, C.G. *Basic Writing.* Congdon and Weed, 1983.

Kaufman, Walter. *Existentialism From Dostoevsky to Sartre.* Meridian Books, 1956.

Lee, Richard. *The !Kung San. Cambridge University* 1979.

Locke, John. *Two Treatises of Government.* Hafner Publishing, 1947.

Maslow, A.H. *Toward a Psychology of Being. D. Van Nostrand, 1962.*

Malinowski, Bronislav. *The Sexual Life of Savages.* Viking Press, 1971.

Mead, Margaret. *Coming of Age in Samoa.* American Museum of Natural History, 1928.

Needham, Joseph. *Science and Civilization in China.* Cambridge University Press 1956.

Neihardt, John. *Black Elk Speacks.* Pocket Books, 1932.

Neill, A.S. *Summerhill.* Hart Publishing, 1960.

Palmer, Martin. *The Book of Chuang Tzu.* Arkana Penguin Books, 1996.

Pelletier, Wilfred. *Two Articles.* Keewin Publishing, 1969.

Pelletier, Wilfred. *For Every North American Indian Who Begins to Disappear/ I also begin to Disappear.* Keewin Publishing, 1971.

Prescott, James. "Body Pleasure and the Origins of Violence" Bulletin of Atomic Scientists, November, 1975.

Reich, Wilhelm. *The Invasion of Compulsory Sex-Morality.* Farrar, Straus and Giroux, 1971.

Reich, Wilhelm. *The Mass Psychology of Fascism.* Farrar, Straus and Giroux 1946.

Reinisch, June. *The Kinsey Institute New Report on Sex. St. Martin's Press, 1990.*

Roscoe, Will. *Living the Spirit.* St. Martin's Press, 1988.

Rouse, W.H.D. *Great Dialogues of Plato.* New American Library, 1956.

Saunders, Trevor. *Plato: The Laws.* Penguin Books, 1970.

Scheurmann, Erich. *The Papalagi.* Real Free Press, 1975.

Snyder, Gary. *The Old Ways.* City Light Books, 1977.

Stone, Merlin. *When Gods was a Woman.* Harvest/HBJ Bokks, 1976.

Storm, Hyemeyohsts. *Seven Arrows.* Ballantine Books 1972.

Turnbull, Colin. *The Forest People.* Simon and Schuster, 1961.

Walker, Barbara. *The Woman's Encyclopedia of Myths and Secrets.* Harper, 1983.

Watson, Burton. *The Complete Works of Chuang-tzu.* Columbia University Press, 1968.

Welch, Holmes. *Taoism: The Parting of the Way.* Beacon Press, 1957.

Wilbur, James. and Allen, Harold. *The Worlds of Plato and Aristotle.* American Books, 1962.

Wilhelm, Richard. *The I-Ching.* Princeton University Press, 1950.

William, Walter. *The Spirit and the Flesh.* Beacon Press, 1986.

Witt, Shirley. and Steiner, Stan. *The Way.* Vintage Books, 1972.

Wu, Yi. *The Book of Lao-tzu.* Great Learning Publishing, 1989.

CPSIA information can be obtained at www.ICGtesting.com
Printed in the USA
LVOW122056171212

312068LV00004B/974/P